# DATE DUE

| | | |
|---|---|---|
| OC 30 '96 | MY 2 3 '00 | JE 5 '07 |
| NO 2 0 '96 | JE 1 0 '00 | NO 1 5 '07 |
| RENEW | | DE 2 1 '07 |
| DE 17 '96 | DE 2 0 '00 | |
| AP 7 '97 | JE 1 1 '01 | |
| MY 1 9 '97 | NO 26 01 | |
| OC 3 '97 | FE 7 '02 | |
| OC 30 '97 | AG 7 02 | |
| MR 30 '99 | | |
| AP 2 8 '99 | AP 4 05 | |
| RENEW | JE 1 1 '07 | |
| MY 2 8 '99 | OC 2 3 03 | |
| MY 2 8 '99 | '8 05 | |
| OV 30 '08 | JE 8 05 | |
| NO 1 2 '99 | NO 2 8 05 | |
| FE 1 0 00 | DE 17 05 | |

DEMCO 38-296

# The
# Affirmative Action
# FRAUD

# The
# Affirmative Action
# FRAUD

## Can We Restore the American Civil Rights Vision?

## *Clint Bolick*

CATO
INSTITUTE
Washington, D.C.

**Library of Congress Cataloging-in-Publication Data**

Bolick, Clint.
    The affirmative action fraud : can we restore the American civil
rights vision? / Clint Bolick.
        p.      cm.
    Includes bibliographical references and index.
    ISBN 1-882577-27-2. — ISBN 1-882577-28-0 (pbk.)
    1. Civil rights—United States.   2. Affirmative action programs—
United States.   I. Title
JC599.U5B556   1996
323′.0973—dc20                                                      95-48393
                                                                         CIP

Cover Design by Mark Fondersmith.

Printed in the United States of America.

CATO INSTITUTE
1000 Massachusetts Ave., N.W.
Washington, D.C. 20001

To Chip Mellor

# Contents

# Acknowledgments

No book is written in a vacuum. In my work and personal relationships, I am very fortunate to interact constantly with extremely bright and talented people whose ideas I admire and shamelessly appropriate. I acknowledge here some particularly weighty debts.

This is my second book collaboration with the Cato Institute, the nation's premier think tank, and I am very proud and fortunate to have its sponsorship. In particular, I appreciate the stalwart support in this endeavor from Ed Crane and David Boaz, two of America's great visionaries. Also I appreciate the constant challenges and helpful edits provided by Roger Pilon, who tries to keep us all intellectually honest. Special thanks to Thomas D. Klingenstein, who provided financial support for the book.

This book is much enriched by contributions from Tricia Penkert and Kelly Clifford, who provided research assistance, and from David Garland and Nina Shokraii, who helped with citations. I am eternally grateful to Keli Luther, not only for her assistance with the manuscript, but more important for her inspiration and encouragement, which sustained me throughout the time I was writing this book.

Over the past few years, several publications have provided valuable outlets for my views on civil rights, and some of the work here builds upon those earlier articles. I am especially appreciative of my very talented friends on the *Wall Street Journal*'s editorial page, and extend special thanks to John Fund and Melanie Kirkpatrick.

My colleagues at the Institute for Justice—Scott Bullock, John Kramer, John Keppler, Rita McLaughlin, Nina Shokraii, Dick Komer (who generously reviewed a draft of the manuscript), Dana Berliner, Donna Matias, Maria Vallecillo, Lynn Mason, Patricia Meyers, and Danny Taglienti—are a constant source of support, inspiration, and humor. They make going to work every day and doing battle in the courts an absolute delight. Special thanks to the Institute's board of directors—David Kennedy, Gerrit Wormhoudt, Manny Klausner,

ACKNOWLEDGMENTS

Jim Lintott, Abigail Thernstrom, and Mark Babunovic—for their constant encouragement and warm friendship.

This book is dedicated to Chip Mellor, who cofounded the Institute for Justice with me and serves as its president and general counsel. Chip hired me out of law school (fortunately he never asked about my grades) to work as an attorney at Mountain States Legal Foundation in Denver. Twelve years ago, we vowed that one day we would join together to launch a public interest law center that would change the world. In September 1991 that dream came true.

Over the years, Chip has been a mentor, partner, godfather to my son Evan, and dear and loyal friend. For all these things I am enormously lucky and forever indebted. With this dedication, I hope I am able to convey just how much this is so.

—Washington, D.C.
October 1995

# Introduction

On April 29, 1992, matters of race and civil rights got up-close and personal.

My colleague Dirk Roggeveen and I arrived in Los Angeles that morning to meet with parents and community activists who were interested in suing the Los Angeles public schools for their appalling failure to provide essential basic educational opportunities to children from low-income families, a condition we believed violated their rights under the California Constitution. Our goal was to secure for these children a "voucher" remedy that would allow their parents to secure a decent education for them outside the failed public school system.

Late that afternoon we met in Compton with the Rev. Matthew Harris, who heads Project Impact, a program that rehabilitates gang members and adolescents who have gotten into serious trouble. Harris favors school vouchers because he believes that to return rehabilitated young people to the festering inner-city public schools from which they came is likely to lose them forever.

Harris had just learned that the Los Angeles police officers who were charged with savagely beating Rodney King had been acquitted. I asked Harris whether there might be trouble that evening, and he thought it quite possible.

Dirk and I both disagreed with the jury's verdict. In fact, only a few weeks earlier, Dirk had joined the Institute for Justice after spending the past several years prosecuting police brutality and racial violence cases with the Civil Rights Division of the U.S. Department of Justice. His former colleagues would later successfully prosecute the officers in a second trial for violating King's civil rights.

But thoughts of imminent violence were far from our minds as we headed in the early evening toward south-central Los Angeles, where we had scheduled a meeting with parents who were prospective plaintiffs in our school choice lawsuit. We enjoyed spirited

1

conversation and rolled down the windows of our rental car to take in the balmy spring air.

As we stopped for a red light a mile or so from our destination in Inglewood, the car abruptly was jolted. I looked across the street and saw several black men throwing rocks at us. The first rock had struck with powerful force just below my open window.

Suddenly one of the men bolted toward us wielding a two-by-four. I quickly locked the door and rolled up the window. The man pounded the car with the board. Because the light was still red, I eased out into oncoming traffic to get past the cars in front of me, and then sped through the intersection to safety.

Though we assumed the attack was a reaction to the Rodney King verdict, we had no comprehension of what was unfolding on the streets around us. As we drove deeper into south-central, Dirk remarked, "As soon as we get to the meeting, we'd better call the police and let them know what's happening."

We arrived at our destination, an office building in a small shopping center, several minutes later. We were greeted by Star Parker, the parent who had organized the meeting. Her look was grave as she ushered us toward a television set, where we saw live helicopter coverage of trucker Reginald Denny, who was being beaten by a mob at the corner of Florence and Normandie only two intersections away. The horror-stricken reporter exclaimed over and over again: "The police have completely pulled out of the area." Dirk and I exchanged anxious looks.

Still we did not fully fathom the danger, and as several parents had braved the disturbances we conducted the meeting anyway. As it broke up after an hour and a half, Star called home and learned that the interstate leading to downtown was closed. If Dirk and I had attempted to return the way we had come, we would have encountered a barricade.

Star offered to lead us to a different route back toward our hotel. As we walked to the parking lot, a car circled menacingly. We later learned that much of the shopping center where the meeting was held was burned to the ground that night.

The drive back to the hotel was harrowing. The irony of Dirk's and my situation stoked my sometimes too-fertile imagination, and I recall mentally composing our obituaries as we navigated toward downtown. I remember vividly at one street corner a fresh-faced young private security guard standing at his post outside a store, obviously terrified. But the police had secured the downtown area just as completely as they had abandoned the outlying neighborhoods. Once I was ensconced safely in a tower of the Westin Bonaventure, I stayed awake most of the night, surveying in horror the conflagration we had so narrowly escaped.

Meanwhile, on the airwaves demagoguery abounded. Police chief Daryl Gates, toward whom I felt an intense desire to inflict violence for betraying his duty to protect the people of south-central Los Angeles, seemed to relish the spectacle of violence perpetrated by blacks and Hispanics against their own communities. Reflecting the opposite extreme, Rep. Maxine Waters characterized the marauders as victims and demanded all manner of new social programs.

For me the events of the evening were palpable and transformative. I had witnessed a complete breakdown of civil order, which I hope never to experience again. Dirk and I were targets of lynch-mob violence solely because we were the wrong color in the wrong place at the wrong time.

But most of all, the experience left me with an intense sense of urgency. It had given me additional insight into a part of American society that most people know little about. From representing inner-city, low-income clients for much of my career as a lawyer, I already had a glimpse of that other America. I knew that many inner-city residents lack basic opportunities most of us take for granted: the opportunity to walk safe streets, to obtain decent schooling for their children, to own a home, and even to earn an honest living. That night I learned something else: when the lives and property of people in poor neighborhoods are in jeopardy, the police do not always respond. And the people who live in those neighborhoods cannot escape, as Dirk and I did. Given those conditions, it is to me much less surprising that Los Angeles erupted than that such cataclysmic upheavals have not occurred much more frequently all across the nation. And in all this, race remains central in hearts and minds on both sides of the divide.

Arrayed against this stark reality our nation's civil rights laws and policies appear utterly impotent. For they are the wrong weapon aimed at the wrong target. If, by a miracle, racial discrimination were eradicated tomorrow, little would change in the lives of the people of south-central Los Angeles or, for that matter, in hundreds

3

of cities all across the United States. Nor does so-called "affirmative action" have the slightest relevance to those people's lives. For those who are isolated in inner cities and plagued with myriad disadvantages, the regime of racial preferences in education, jobs, and contracting that passes for affirmative action has little salience. For that reason I call affirmative action "trickle-down" civil rights: benefits are bestowed upon the most-advantaged members of designated groups in the name of the least-advantaged, who somehow never seem to reap those benefits.

What many of the civil rights policies of the past three decades have done, however, is to reinforce the propensity of individuals to define themselves in terms of their race. That consequence is ironic, because the civil rights laws ostensibly are aimed at overcoming past discrimination and moving toward a color-blind society. But it is not surprising, because anytime opportunities are allocated on the basis of race and gender, and political lines are drawn on the basis of group identity, the result is heightened race-consciousness. And inevitably the process will cause a powerful backlash among those who believe they are losing out.

Affirmative action perhaps is unique among entitlement programs in that few perceive themselves as beneficiaries, while many perceive themselves as victims. And because it is a uniquely race-based entitlement, its divisiveness eats like cancer at the national fabric.

My first exposure to the issue occurred during college, when I battled with my university president over racial preferences in faculty hiring. As a product of a working-class family who worked his way through school, I believed it was a manifest injustice for people to gain benefits on the basis not of merit or disadvantage but of skin color. My interest intensified during law school at the University of California at Davis, a citadel of political correctness and the site of the first major U.S. Supreme Court battle over racial quotas, *Regents of the University of California v. Bakke.*[1]

As a lawyer fresh out of law school, I joined Mountain States Legal Foundation in Denver, where I sought Supreme Court review in cases representing victims of racial quotas who had lost their lawsuits in lower courts. (At that time, virtually all court decisions upheld racial preferences.) One of these cases, *Wygant v. Jackson Board of Education,*[2] was the first in which a majority of the Supreme Court applied the most stringent standard of judicial review to cases

4

of reverse discrimination, striking down a racial quota for teacher layoffs in Flint, Michigan.

Before long I succumbed to the siren call of Washington. The Reagan administration had been waging an all-out offensive against racial preferences in the courts, and I enlisted first at the U.S. Equal Employment Opportunity Commission (1985–86) and then in the Civil Rights Division of the U.S. Department of Justice (1986–87).

I came to Washington to fight quotas, but I was nudged gently in a different direction by my mentors at the EEOC, Chairman Clarence Thomas and Commissioner Ricky Silberman. Though they agreed with the ideal of a color-blind Constitution, they were less concerned with the plight of white firefighters victimized by reverse discrimination than with those who had been left behind by the civil rights revolution. They encouraged me to develop alternative strategies to help empower people outside the economic mainstream. Before long I came to view these approaches—eradicating government race and gender preferences and promoting individual empowerment—as two sides of the same coin.

But real headway on these issues at the time seemed nearly impossible. Those who waged the civil rights battles of the 1950s and '60s had earned a powerful claim to the moral high ground. Sadly, two decades later many of the former revolutionaries had abandoned the principles they once had championed, but still they had a moral monopoly over civil rights. This civil rights establishment fiercely suppressed any meaningful discussion about competing civil rights philosophies or strategies. John Jacob, president of the National Urban League, gave definition to the establishment's dogma in a 1985 speech: "The goal of parity between the races," he pronounced, "is the one constant that must be shared by anyone who presumes to hold a leadership position in the black community."[3] Anyone who dared question the prevailing orthodoxy was denounced as racist if white or an "Uncle Tom" if black.

In the late 1980s, I wrote two books, *Changing Course: Civil Rights at the Crossroads*[4] and *Unfinished Business: A Civil Rights Strategy for America's Third Century.*[5] Like the handful of other books written at the time questioning conventional wisdom on civil rights issues, these books largely were ignored, especially by the civil rights establishment. Surprisingly, the *Washington Post* reviewed *Unfinished Business.* But the review was devastating, offering nary a kind word about the book.[6] When I expressed disappointment, my colleague Steve Eagle helped me place it in perspective. "Clint," he told me, "before this book review, the civil rights groups considered you beneath contempt. Now you've risen to the level of contempt."

Fortunately, around this same time, other dissenting voices began to be raised against the prevailing orthodoxy. William Julius Wilson,[7] Stephen Carter,[8] and Shelby Steele[9] questioned the efficacy of race-based affirmative action programs. Meanwhile, pioneers like Jack Kemp, Bob Woodson of the National Center for Neighborhood Enterprise, and Wisconsin State Rep. Polly Williams began exploring race-neutral ways to bring society's outsiders into the mainstream by giving people greater power to control their own destinies (I explore some of these ideas in Chapter 10).

At the same time, I began to develop a civil rights litigation program designed to eliminate barriers to opportunity, focusing on the efforts of low-income people to gain greater entrepreneurial and educational opportunities. Over the past eight years, mainly at the Institute for Justice, these efforts have yielded such successes as opening entry-level opportunities into the taxicab industry in Denver, Indianapolis, and Cincinnati, and into the cosmetology profession in Washington, D.C.; overturning a ban on "jitney" transit services in Houston; and defending the nation's first private school choice program in Milwaukee. Unlike race-preference programs, these efforts are not racially divisive, even though the people who benefit are primarily minorities. That is because these efforts focus on opening opportunities to the economically disadvantaged, rather than redistributing opportunities on the basis of race.

Unfortunately, elected officials at the national level so far have not seized the opportunity to forge a new civil rights consensus along these lines. Indeed, civil rights issues all but disappeared during the 1992 campaign. George Bush capitulated on the issue of race preferences when he signed the Civil Rights Act of 1991, which previously he had denounced as a "quota bill"; and he failed to present any coherent alternative (see Chapter 8).[10] By contrast, candidate Bill Clinton was able to lure disaffected Democrats back into the fold, promising new thinking on race issues. In high-profile confrontations, he criticized rap singer Sister Souljah for her racist lyrics and denounced "bean counters" and "quota games." A truly "new Democrat" seemed to have arrived in the White House.

But instead, the Clinton administration has relentlessly pursued divisive race-based policies and has done nothing to look for common ground or new approaches to civil rights issues (see Chapter 7). The administration's direction was personified by law professor Lani Guinier, President Clinton's first nominee as Assistant Attorney General for Civil Rights, the nation's top civil rights law enforcement post. I was alerted to the imminent nomination by Boston University professor Abigail Thernstrom, who urged me to read Guinier's writings. When I did, I was dismayed: Guinier painted a bleak view of an American society permeated by race-consciousness and discrimination. Her prescribed remedies were more radical than any I had previously encountered, and seemed to me a recipe for a society permanently divided into hostile racial camps (see Chapter 6).

In response, I authored two op-ed articles in the *Wall Street Journal* calling attention to Guinier's views,[11] and the Institute for Justice disseminated dozens of verbatim copies of her law review articles, urging journalists and policymakers to read them in their entirety. Most of those who did so—ultimately including the president himself—concluded that Guinier should not be entrusted with the nation's mighty civil rights law enforcement apparatus.

Sadly but predictably, Guinier's supporters in the civil rights establishment responded not by defending her views but by engaging in *ad hominem* attacks (my favorite was one by professor Pat Williams, who denounced me in *Village Voice* as a "wacky, fun-loving knucklehead"), or by denying Guinier had said what was attributed to her. Indeed, Guinier herself edited out significant controversial passages in her subsequently published collection of supposedly verbatim law review articles.[12] Though Guinier repeatedly has called for a "dialogue" on race issues, she consistently refuses to debate me or other informed critics.[13]

Later, when I suggested that Deval Patrick, Clinton's subsequent nominee for the civil rights post, was a "stealth Guinier,"[14] the president himself led the counterattack. In a podium-thumping diatribe reminiscent of Nikita Khrushchev, Clinton fired an assault at those who dared question the nomination:

> They never believed in civil rights laws, they never believed in equal opportunity, they never lifted a finger to give anybody of a minority race a chance in this country.... If they attack his record, it means just exactly what we've suspected all along: They don't give a rip about civil rights.[15]

7

Despite the best efforts of President Clinton and the civil rights establishment to silence debate, the broad-based opposition to Guinier's nomination exposed the strong passions about race-based policies that have been simmering for some time just beneath the surface of American politics. Those passions have been rekindled by a series of events: the Clinton administration's civil rights policies, the whole of which demonstrates that the Guinier nomination was no aberration; the California Civil Rights Initiative, aimed at eliminating race and gender preferences in state government; the election of a new generation of Republicans to a majority in Congress; and legislative efforts to curb racial preferences in the federal government.

These influences have combined to open an unprecedented debate over civil rights policies, fueled by public opinion polls showing that large majorities of Americans of all colors and ethnicities oppose racial preferences. For the first time, establishment civil rights leaders are conceding that "excesses" or "mistakes" may have occurred that require correction; and a growing number of liberal commentators suggest that race-based affirmative action should cease.[16] Meanwhile, some supporters of the status quo, unable to defend morally bankrupt policies, are resorting to fanning the flames of racial hatred.

That response is unfortunate. No policies, no matter how beneficent their purpose, are infallible. Sometimes policies that are appropriate to one time are inappropriate to another. Any policies that cannot stand the test of critical reexamination ought to be suspect, and race-conscious "affirmative action" policies have never been seriously examined over 30 years of constant proliferation. I am glad to see that many who previously considered the status quo sacrosanct now are acknowledging the need to reconsider conventional wisdom. But I believe that a sweeping change in our nation's civil rights agenda is necessary to begin the process of racial healing and to secure for all Americans the opportunities to which they are entitled.

How might we go about this broad and daunting task? It seems to me the place to start is with the core principles underlying the American civil rights vision. Most histories of the civil rights movement in America start in the 1950s or '60s, as if little or nothing anteceded the modern civil rights movement.

But the quest for civil rights in America started much earlier than that. It started in 1776, when the American colonists declared their independence from Britain and proclaimed the inalienable rights of all individuals to life, liberty, and the pursuit of happiness.

Tragically, our nation from the outset betrayed these principles. And so there began a movement to make good on America's moral commitment to civil rights. Its first object was the abolition of slavery, which culminated in the guarantee of equality under law and fundamental liberties for all Americans. From that time until the 1960s, the movement was focused on securing basic rights for Americans who were denied them. The 1954 *Brown v. Board of Education*[17] decision by the U.S. Supreme Court seemed to presage an end to government's power to classify its citizens on the basis of race or to deny equal opportunities.

Anyone studying the civil rights movement from its genesis in our nation's infancy through the 1960s will be struck by the clarity and consistency of the moral vision adhered to by the movement's leaders through nearly two centuries—and struck by the sudden and complete abandonment of that vision since the '60s. In place of the vision that fueled the movement's great triumphs is a revised agenda that substitutes individual rights with group entitlements, color-blindness with race-consciousness, freedom with coercion. The concept of civil rights has been transformed from those basic rights we share as Americans into special privileges for some and burdens for others. As a consequence, Americans are as racially divided as ever, with not nearly enough tangible progress.

Before we can move forward, we must confront an important question: how did we get in the position in which we find ourselves today? After the great triumphs for civil rights such a short time ago, how did we rush back into the abyss of racial division? To extricate ourselves from this mire, we need to understand fully the reasons for, and nature of, our present predicament.

This book places our contemporary challenges in their historical context by tracing the evolution, principles, and accomplishments of the civil rights movement since our nation's founding and examining both the underpinnings and consequences of the revised agenda that supplanted the original civil rights vision. Finally, it sketches a strategy to restore the American civil rights vision and to fulfill its great promise.

It is this latter aspect—a positive civil rights strategy—that I consider most important by far. Because the Institute for Justice and I have received a disproportionate share of our public visibility on affirmative action and related issues, it sometimes comes as a surprise that principally we are not lobbyists but litigators, and that the people we represent are not white victims of reverse discrimination but mainly low-income people seeking greater economic or educational opportunities. In these pages you will meet some of the people I have been privileged to represent in the courtroom over the past eight years. Their stories help personalize what often are abstract yet emotionally charged issues and demonstrate why, in human terms, we need urgently to chart a positive new course for civil rights. Frankly, although I think the issue of racial preferences is very important, if forced to choose I would trade it in a heartbeat for greater individual empowerment, such as school choice and economic liberty (see Chapter 10). In fact, such efforts could render moot the whole debate over racial preferences.

Ultimately, I am convinced we can restore forward momentum in the quest for civil rights only by reclaiming our nation's founding principles. And, as was the case with the nation's great civil rights leaders, by applying those principles to contemporary realities.

The time is long overdue for our nation to make good on its promise of equal opportunity, as recent events make painfully clear. The polarized reaction to the O. J. Simpson verdict—blacks overwhelmingly supporting acquittal, whites believing him guilty— revealed a racial chasm much wider than most people realized. Blacks and whites too often see the world through race-tinted prisms of divergent experiences, and think of themselves not as individuals but as members of groups. That will continue so long as government classifies individuals on the basis of race, and so long as the pathway to the American Dream is blocked for many members of our society. To bridge the racial divide, we need urgently to curb government's power to discriminate, and to provide for Americans of all colors a common experience.

These are revolutionary times—times in which what previously was unthinkable is now thinkable, and what previously was impossible is now possible. We finally can deliver on our nation's most sacred commitments: to judge individuals on the content of their character and not the color of their skin; to invest all individuals with the right to life, liberty, and the pursuit of happiness. If we fail to do so, we may never have such a chance again.

# 1. Civil Rights Conundrum

The current state of civil rights in America can be seen in the stories of Mark and James, two little boys coming of age in the 1990s. Mark and James have a lot in common: both are black, growing up in midwestern inner cities, with loving families who care deeply about their futures.

Except for these similarities, however, their circumstances could hardly be more different. For Mark Anthony Nevels, the future looked bright when his parents were preparing to enroll him in kindergarten. Right across the street from his home was Weeks Elementary School, which had been transformed into a high-quality "magnet" school as a result of a desegregation order governing the Kansas City public schools. Mark's parents were delighted over the prospect of sending him to a good school to which he could walk easily, and where they could be involved closely in his education.

But when Mark's family tried to enroll him, they were shocked to learn he could not be admitted despite the fact that the school had plenty of space. It turns out that the same desegregation decree contained an explicit racial quota: for every two white children who enrolled, three black children could be admitted. When Mark attempted to enroll, only four white children had chosen to attend, meaning only six black students would be admitted. The result was that in a kindergarten with space for 122 youngsters, only 10 spaces would be filled—and 112 seats held empty, despite a waiting list containing 86 black children, including Mark.

So as he started his formal schooling, Mark faced this prospect: instead of attending an excellent school across the street from his home, every morning he would have to board a school bus, ride past his neighborhood school, and attend an inferior school farther away, and he would have to do this because he was black.

If this scenario sounds hauntingly familiar, perhaps it is because it presents precisely the same set of facts raised by the 1954 case,

*Brown v. Board of Education*[1]: black children bused past their neighborhood schools to inferior schools solely on account of race. Which raises a very sobering question: have we traveled so far and painful a distance in 40 years only to end up in precisely the same place we started?

For James, the beginning looked far more dismal than it appeared for Mark. James spent the first three years of his schooling in the Milwaukee public schools, a dreadful environment but very typical of the circumstances facing children from low-income families in inner-city public school districts all around the nation. In Milwaukee, children from families on public assistance had an 85 percent dropout rate. Those few who graduated had a "D" grade-point average. The schools were filled with crime and disruption. For youngsters like James, the odds were much greater that they would drop out of school, become welfare dependent, or become criminals or victims of crime, than that they would graduate and go on to college or productive livelihoods.

But when James was in second grade, something happened to change that bleak equation. A little revolution took place, led by Annette "Polly" Williams, a black state legislator and former welfare mother. Williams in 1990 successfully sponsored the Milwaukee Parental Choice Program, the nation's first private school choice program. As initially enacted, the program allowed up to 1,000 low-income children to leave failing public schools and to use their share of state education funds—about $2,500 per student—as full payment of tuition in nonsectarian community private schools.

So instead of having to attend an educational cesspool, James could attend a neighborhood private school, boasting a safe and positive educational environment and a 95 percent graduation rate—a school chosen by his parents.

The school choice program had a dramatic impact not only on children like James but also on the entire school system and on public schooling nationwide. For the first time, power over essential educational decisions was transferred from bureaucrats to parents. And perhaps even more important, public schools were forced to *compete* for low-income students and the education funds they commanded.

Not surprisingly, both the Kansas City racial quota[2] and the Milwaukee school choice program[3] wound up in court. And predictably, civil rights groups were involved in both lawsuits. But not on the side of their supposed constituents: in Kansas City, the civil rights groups not only defended but were the architects of the racial quota that kept Mark out of Weeks Elementary School; and in Wisconsin, the Milwaukee chapter of the National Association for the Advancement of Colored People was the lead plaintiff challenging the constitutionality of the school choice program.

That groups claiming to support civil rights would find themselves anywhere other than shoulder-to-shoulder with Mark and James in their fight for educational opportunities speaks volumes about the civil rights schizophrenia that wracks our nation. These all-too-typical examples illustrate the chasm that has grown between today's self-proclaimed civil rights leaders and the people they claim to represent. Black youngsters like Mark and James, in whose name the civil rights revolution was fought, are now sacrificed by their self-proclaimed champions in the service of social engineering and special interest politics. As it has descended from the lofty heights of a civil rights revolution into a frenzied struggle for racial entitlements, the civil rights establishment has ceded the moral high ground and trivialized the very concept of civil rights.

The consequences of this abdication of principles are widespread and devastating. They affect every one of us, personally and directly. A nation that prides itself on being a well-assimilated "melting pot" has retreated into a kind of modern apartheid system, in which our color, race, ethnicity, and gender increasingly determine our rights and opportunities—and, as a consequence, our identities and the way we perceive each other. And this 30 years after the supposed triumph of a civil rights movement that was doctrinally committed to individualism and color-blindness.

Those who occupy the civil rights establishment often are contemptuous of those who criticize the status quo. If white males suffer discrimination, they assert, that is only what they deserve after 200 years of slavery and other injustices. But discrimination is discrimination, and it hurts no less when one's skin color is white. Race-based affirmative action, says Lovida Coleman, an attorney and daughter of William Coleman, one of the architects of preferences, "is imposing the same kind of indignation among white people that we so deeply resented for so many years: The anguish of being told the color of your skin means no."[4]

13

But as the examples at the beginning of this chapter demonstrate, counting by race eventually harms or stigmatizes everyone, even its purported beneficiaries. As Shelby Steele declares, "Race should not be a source of power or advantage or disadvantage for anyone in a free society."[5]

Yet race-consciousness has become deeply embedded in our national policy. Some measure of this is reflected in Directive 15, adopted by the federal Office of Management and Budget (OMB) in 1977. Directive 15 instructs federal agencies to collect statistics identifying people within five racial and ethnic categories: American Indian or Alaskan Native, Asian or Pacific Islander, Black, Hispanic, or White. "For purposes of reporting on persons who are of mixed racial and/or ethnic origins," the directive states, the "category which most closely reflects the individual's recognition in his community should be used." In addition to statistical purposes, OMB reports that "some important examples of the Federal Government's uses of racial and ethnic data are

- enforcing the requirements of the Voting Rights Act;
- reviewing State redistricting plans; . . .
- establishing and evaluating Federal affirmative action plans and evaluating affirmative action in employment in the private sector; . . .
- monitoring and enforcing desegregation plans in the public schools;
- assisting minority businesses under the minority business development programs; and
- monitoring and enforcing the Fair Housing Act."[6]

The use of race and gender to distribute opportunities is so pervasive that a study by the Congressional Research Service in January 1995 identified 160 federal government programs employing explicit race and gender criteria.[7] That number is multiplied exponentially by programs at the state and local levels, as well as by private companies and educational institutions subject to the civil rights laws.

Nor, as Directive 15 suggests, is official race-consciousness limited to so-called affirmative action in employment or education. Defenders of the status quo often claim such programs have a limited real-world impact. In fact, official race classifications touch each and every one of our lives, not only through affirmative action but through race-conscious policies affecting school district boundaries, pupil assignment in public schools, electoral line-drawing, scholarship programs, public housing, jury selection, credit opportunities, the use of tests in employment and education, small business loans, and myriad other regulations both sweeping and trivial. In each of these areas, our identification within a particular group determines in some measure our obligations or opportunities.

It is therefore little wonder that increasingly we look at each other not as individuals or as Americans, but as members of groups. In a multiethnic society founded on the credo of individualism—consisting increasingly of individuals who themselves are multi-ethnic—this is particularly vexing. "Today our country may be more of a genetic melting pot than at any time in history," observes columnist Ellen Goodman. "Yet we are often and oppositely as obsessed with racial and ethnic categories as any 19th century census taker," she laments. "More often than not we ask of some subtle shading, some 'exotic' feature: 'What is he?' 'What is she?' Not who, mind you, but what."[8]

A colleague of mine tells the story of ethnic categorization by a law firm where she was employed in San Francisco. My colleague is half-Filipino, half-Caucasian, and has a Spanish-sounding surname. After she started working at the law firm, she received phone calls soliciting participation in Hispanic attorney associations. She explained she was not Hispanic, and when she asked where the groups had obtained her name, she was told that her law firm's personnel office made the referral. Later, she confronted the personnel official about how such erroneous information was generated, as she never had been asked her ethnicity. "Oh," replied the personnel official, "when we don't know, we do a 'visual'." Undaunted by the embarrassing situation, the official pressed my colleague to identify herself within a group. "Well, I'm half-Caucasian," my colleague replied, "so why don't you just list me as white?" Somehow, I don't think that's what the personnel official wanted to hear.

My colleague probably suffered no more than minor indignity (and perhaps derived perverse amusement) from this incident, but in many cases the consequences of racial classifications are not so harmless. And in no sense are those consequences always positive for members of what the civil rights establishment likes to call "protected groups."

Take the case of two young brothers, Matthew and Joseph.[9] Matthew was born four years ago addicted to crack cocaine and infected with syphilis. He immediately came under the control of the Texas Department of Protective and Regulatory Services (DPRS), which placed him at nine days old in the care of Scott and Lou Ann Mullen, whose adopted, foster, and natural family includes members of white, black, Native American, Hispanic, and mixed-race origins.

Scott and Lou Ann nurtured Matthew to health and fell in love with him. But when they announced to the social workers their desire to adopt Matthew, they were told they would not be allowed to do so because Matthew was black and the Mullens were not. When Matthew was two, DPRS removed him from the Mullens' home to an adoptive placement in a black family with his older brother, Joseph. The placement fell apart. The Mullens decided to try to adopt both boys, but even after DPRS placed both boys in the family's foster care, it continued to search for a same-race placement. Only after the Institute for Justice filed a class-action lawsuit to enforce Texas law prohibiting discrimination in adoption placements did DPRS relent and allow Matthew and Joseph to become a permanent part of the Mullens' loving home.

That story is repeated every day throughout the nation. Forty-three states have laws permitting or requiring "race matching" in state adoptive placements.[10] Even in states like Texas that prohibit such practices, social workers thwart the laws and pursue same-race adoptions even if the practice requires keeping children in foster or institutional arrangements. Because a disproportionate share— more than 50 percent—of children awaiting adoption belong to minority groups, the insistence of state welfare workers on seeking same-race adoptions often subjects minority children to lengthy delays and multiple placements even though loving adoptive families await them.

The problem stems from a resolution by the National Association of Black Social Workers (NABSW), dating back to the 1970s, that terms interracial adoptions "cultural genocide." NABSW's militant position, a throwback to the racial purity ideology of the Jim Crow era, has permeated the social worker profession and led to an apartheid system of adoption placements. As with all race-based ideologies, NABSW's has bizarre permutations: biracial children are deemed "black," while biracial couples are considered "white," so that couples might not be able to adopt children who look like their own—all in the name of preserving racial "identity."

From my experience battling barriers to interracial adoptions I have learned one enduring lesson: any exception to the principle of color-blindness, no matter how narrow, will be pried open wide enough to drive a truck through. That is a conclusion supported by more than 200 years of American history, and by all too many contemporary examples. Indeed, even though we already have on the books a series of constitutional precedents in which the U.S. Supreme Court has ruled that government may use racial classifications only for the most compelling justifications, and then only in the narrowest of ways,[11] such race and gender classifications continue to proliferate at every level of government.

The architects of the current regime of race-consciousness have introduced into our polity a number of poisonous concepts. One is that merit sometimes has to give way to immutable group characteristics such as race or gender. It is true, of course, that despite our society's professed commitment to meritocracy, we often deviate from that standard. The "old boy" network, preferences for the sons and daughters of college alumni, political spoils systems—all reward the well-connected over newcomers and outsiders, and all of us who hail from humble origins have had to overcome them. In a nation committed to equal opportunity, it seems absolutely essential that we eschew such deviations from the merit principle, and instead work assiduously to level the playing field, a task I address in greater detail in Chapter 10.

But is there any less-useful way to redress these instances of unfairness than by means of racial preferences? That is the crudest possible means to provide justice, for members of the preferred groups are not in equal measure affected by such barriers; and preferences are racially divisive and reinforcing of the habit of thinking about each other in terms of race. But much more debilitating is the message it delivers to its supposed beneficiaries: you do not have to hold yourself to the highest possible standards of excellence; we will excuse and reward you even if you are mediocre. What a patronizing approach, which reinforces notions of racial inferiority— at such variance with the teachings of great civil rights leaders such as Frederick Douglass, Booker T. Washington, W. E. B. DuBois, and the Rev. Martin Luther King Jr. "Progress in the enjoyment of all

17

the privileges that will come to us must be the result of severe and constant struggle rather than of artificial forcing," Booker T. Washington emphasized. "No race that has anything to contribute to the markets of the world is long in any degree ostracized."[12]

The architects of the status quo have introduced a second related poisonous concept: that group identity influences how individuals think (or, more ominously, how they *should* think). This position leads logically to conclusions its proponents certainly should not wish to entertain: if race determines a person's thoughts, then why does it not determine a person's intelligence? Notions of group-think inherently undermine a system that treats people as individuals, and give justification to those who would treat groups differently— regardless of whether the motivations are benign or malevolent.

The latest manifestation of this concept is the movement to foster "diversity," which in this Orwellian mindset actually means conformity. As is often the case, the frontlines in this crusade are the universities, where ancestry and pigmentation join with ideology to determine who is "authentically" black for diversity purposes (a theme to which I will return in my discussion of Lani Guinier in Chapter 6). The *Wall Street Journal's* Melanie Kirkpatrick reported the all-too-typical example of Northwestern Law School in Chicago, which wanted to retain one of its black law professors, Keith Hylton.[13] But a competing law school, Boston University, offered positions to both Hylton and his wife, Maria, who was teaching law at DePaul University. Northwestern asked the couple to defer a decision until it could try to arrange a position for Maria Hylton as well.

This effort set off a tempest among the faculty at Northwestern. Leading the assault, a black professor, Joyce Hughes, fired off a memorandum contending that Maria Hylton "should not be considered a Black candidate" because her parents were a black Cuban and a white Australian. Moreover, Hughes argued, the addition of Maria Hylton would mean most of the law school's minority professors were not philosophically liberal, which mattered because black students at the law school needed minority professors who would "validate" them. "If a law school has an ample number of minorities as professors," Hughes wrote, "then conflicting viewpoints among them could be instructive"; but otherwise, only the orthodox liberal black viewpoint should be presented. In the end, Hughes succeeded in preserving her cherished intellectual homogeneity: the Hyltons accepted the teaching offers in Boston.

Ironically, it was in Boston a few years ago that following a particularly hostile student forum I met a young black philosophy student. He informed me that there are only a handful of black students in philosophy doctoral programs nationwide, and described the intense pressure on him from fellow black students to switch to "Black Studies" or some other non-"European" program.

These incidents make an important point that many opponents of racial preferences sometimes fail adequately to grasp: that ours is still not a colorblind society. The color line remains an omnipresent fact of American life.

Yet they illustrate as well that, increasingly, the color line stems, not only from our history and from ongoing discrimination, but also from the choices individuals make. We have eradicated official segregation in higher education, yet many minority students segregate themselves into separate dormitories and academic programs. Even as black candidates like former governor Doug Wilder and Sen. Carol Moseley-Braun win large numbers of white votes and white politicians like Jack Kemp and Gov. Tommy Thompson attract strong black support, voters still tend strongly to back candidates of their own race when that choice arises. Looking at identical evidence, a large majority of whites thought O. J. Simpson was guilty, while an equally large majority of blacks thought he was innocent.[14]

All this is not necessarily troublesome. Inherent in a free society is the liberty to choose one's associations, including the right to choose to associate with people who are most like ourselves. The football player Jim Brown was paraphrased in the 1960s as saying "he personally wouldn't want to live with whites but that he damned well wanted to know that he could if he did want to."[15] The point is that government should not place barriers in the way of individuals' freedom to choose.

But the color line goes deeper than that. How much so I never fully appreciated until a lunch I shared a few years ago with a reporter who was one of the first blacks to break into the ranks of mainstream journalism. He was also the first major reporter to cover in the late 1980s my newly launched civil rights litigation program, and since that time we have become friends. Over lunch, he described how he was married to a white woman, the father of a mixed-race daughter, and a resident in an integrated, mostly white neighborhood. And yet, he told me, "There is not a single day, or a single hour within the day, when I do not think of my blackness."

This comment struck me powerfully. I almost never think about my "whiteness." My European roots are so distant and amorphous that I feel no ethnic identification whatsoever other than American. Can we ever reach the point in our society when individuals truly can be judged by the content of their character and not by the color of their skin? Are we so far down the road of race-consciousness that race and ethnicity are the primary determinants of how we perceive ourselves and others? Is the melting pot a lost ideal?

Defenders of the status quo constantly invoke the continuing existence of discrimination and the failure to achieve a colorblind society as evidence that we continue to need race-conscious social policies. It seems to me the conclusion contradicts the premise. Though the task of building a society consistent with the American ideals of individualism and equal opportunity is by no means an easy one, one thing is certain: the one way we can ensure that we *never* achieve a colorblind society is to continue classifying individuals on the basis of race, ethnicity, and gender.

But those who seek to eradicate such distinctions need also to acknowledge a second grim reality: despite our nation's commitment to equal opportunity, millions of Americans are far removed from the most basic opportunities, and the condition of disadvantage correlates strongly with race.

Of course, in many respects, minorities have experienced impressive advances. As economist Peter M. Drucker relates,

> In the 50 years since the Second World War, the economic position of African-Americans has improved faster than that of any other group in American social history—or in the social history of any country. Three-fifths of America's blacks rose to middle-class incomes; before the Second World War the figure was one-twentieth.[16]

Yet the statistics along an entire array of economic and social criteria are sobering. According to the National Urban League, the median net household worth for black families in 1988 was $4,169, compared to $43,279 for white families. Over 29 percent of black families had zero or negative net worth, compared with 8.7 percent of white families; only 5.2 percent of black families had net worths above $100,000, contrasted with 29.2 percent of white families.[17] In 1992, 33.3 percent of all blacks were below the poverty level, compared to 11.6 percent of whites.[18] In 1991, the black unemployment rate was 12.4 percent, more than twice as high as the white unemployment rate.[19] The black-to-white unemployment gap has actually widened between 1964 and today.[20]

Likewise, the Urban League reports that blacks are 6.4 times more likely to die by homicide than whites.[21] In 1991, 46.4 percent of all black families were headed by single females[22]—a figure that has doubled since 1960.[23] In 1970, 38 percent of black births were out-of-wedlock; by 1988, that number had grown to 64 percent. By the year 2000, the proportion of black children living with both parents is predicted to decline to 24 percent.[24] For these children, the odds are great for a life of poverty.

Educational prospects are equally bleak: in 1991, 19.6 percent of blacks between the ages of 20 and 29 did not have a high school diploma, and an additional 46.4 percent did not progress beyond high school.[25] The National Assessment of Educational Progress in 1995 reported that only 12 percent of black high school seniors (as compared to a dismal-enough 40 percent of whites) were proficient in reading.[26] According to Shelby Steele, 72 percent of black college students drop out.[27] The educational statistics manifest themselves in additional ways: as many as three-fourths of black males between the ages of 25 to 34 who dropped out of high school had criminal records.[28] Overall, nearly one of every three black men between the ages of 20 and 29 is in jail or otherwise under supervision of the judicial system, which represents a 30 percent increase since 1989.[29]

These statistics yield at least two major ramifications for civil rights policies. First, statistical disparities—differences in outcomes among groups—can no longer readily be attributed to discrimination. So long as vast proportions of minorities do not gain high school diplomas, or are locked inside the walls of poverty, it is unlikely they are in a position to compete effectively for jobs, college admissions, or contracting opportunities. In other words, so long as these bleak social and educational patterns persist, we can expect that, all things being equal, minorities will be significantly under-represented, relative to their population, in most walks of mainstream life.

Closely related is a second ramification: traditional civil rights remedies do not hold much hope for the truly disadvantaged. As political scientist Seymour Martin Lipset observes, "Whatever the causes of childhood poverty, affirmative action is no remedy for this group. Preference policies or quotas are not much help to an illegitimate black ghetto youth who grows up in poverty and receives an inferior education."[30] Race-conscious affirmative action is relevant only to those who are eligible for job, business, or college opportunities—and utterly irrelevant to the remainder.

If it is true that discrimination no longer explains many or most of these disadvantages, then we urgently need to determine the nature of the remaining barriers to opportunity and eradicate them. It seems clear that massive welfare programs and the race-specific policies of the past 30 years, despite their enormous costs, both economic and social, are not up to the task of bringing large numbers of economic outsiders into the mainstream of American life.

So we have twin dilemmas: civil rights policies, designed to ensure that Americans will be judged on the basis of individual merit, now increasingly divide people by race; and millions of Americans remaining separated from essential opportunities. In the pages that follow I will confront those dilemmas in turn and suggest that the solution to each—or, at the least, a key requisite to solving each—is the rediscovery of essential lost principles. It is to identifying those principles—embodied in the American civil rights vision—that the next chapter is devoted.

# 2. First Principles

> It is at all times necessary ... that we frequently refresh our patriotism by reference to first principles. It is by tracing things to their origin that we learn to understand them; and it is by keeping that line and origin always in view that we never forget them.
>
> —Thomas Paine, *Dissertation on First Principles of Government* (1775)

> [I]n a real sense, America is essentially a dream, a dream as yet unfulfilled.... The substance of the dream is expressed in these sublime words, lifted to cosmic proportions: "We hold these truths to be self-evident, that all men are created equal, that they are endowed by their Creator with certain unalienable rights, that among these are life, liberty, and the pursuit of happiness." This is the dream.
>
> — Martin Luther King Jr. (1961)[1]

All of us, at some time or another, have discussed or argued about "civil rights." The term is familiar to every American, prominent in political discourse, and the stuff of myriad lawsuits.

Yet ask people to define "civil rights" and you likely will evoke mumbled responses and bewildered stares. Some people think that opposition to preferential treatment is tantamount to opposition to civil rights. Others define any injustice, unfairness, or personal indignity as a violation of civil rights. The perception is widespread that civil rights are a matter of concern to some groups and not to others and that they consist largely of entitlements justified as a form of reparation for past discrimination and social inequality.

Those notions are stoked consciously and consistently by those who style themselves today's civil rights leaders. Mary Frances Berry, whom President Clinton elevated to the chair of the U.S. Commission on Civil Rights, has taken the position that "[c]ivil rights laws were not passed to give civil rights protections to all

23

Americans," but just to members of certain groups.[2] Establishment civil rights organizations like the National Association for the Advancement of Colored People (NAACP) and National Urban League assert a "right" to jobs, health care, and housing; others, like the NAACP Legal Defense and Educational Fund and the Lawyers' Committee for Civil Rights, litigate regularly in support of racial quotas, forced busing, and gerrymandered voting districts. Little wonder that many people perceive civil rights as an us-versus-them proposition.

That was not always so. The civil rights movement in America traces its origins back more than 200 years. It has had as its main objective the fulfillment of civil rights for all Americans. In that quest the civil rights movement set itself two overarching tasks: in its first century, abolishing slavery; in the second century, providing equal opportunity. Throughout those two centuries, the underlying mission and principles were clear and consistent. Every great civil rights advocate from Tom Paine to William Lloyd Garrison to Frederick Douglass to Booker T. Washington to Martin Luther King Jr. shared a common vision, a common set of goals and ideals. It is that shared agenda that I shall refer to throughout this book as the American civil rights vision.[3]

In this civil rights vision, the definition of civil rights is simple and straightforward: civil rights are those basic rights we all share equally as members of civil society. Indeed, our nation's moral claim is staked in its doctrinal commitment to civil rights, which accounts in no small measure for the boundless passion and effort that countless people have committed to fulfill that commitment. Moreover, adherence to this vision consistently fueled the civil rights movement's greatest triumphs, while deviations from the vision during the past 30 years have produced the ambivalence and confusion with which many Americans view civil rights today.

A thorough examination of the history of civil rights in America yields four themes that are essential to understanding the American civil rights vision:

- First, civil rights are inherently *individual* rights, defined essentially as the right to life, liberty, and the pursuit of happiness.
- Second, these rights are held *equally* under law.
- Third, civil rights are *universal*, belonging to every individual.

- Fourth, these rights consist not of material entitlements but essential *liberties*; that is, freedom from coercion.

That classical liberal vision of civil rights* traces its roots to the fertile philosophical soil of the American Revolution. The foundations of the new republic were built on the philosophy of "natural rights." As Martin Luther King Jr. would observe nearly 200 years later, the founders "took from John Locke of England the theory of natural rights and the justification of revolution and imbued it with the ideal of a society governed by the people."[4]

The United States was the first nation founded on natural rights principles. As the historian Lord Acton observed,

> Europe seemed incapable of becoming the home of free States. It was from America that the plain ideas that men ought to mind their own business, and that the nation is responsible to Heaven for the acts of the State—ideas long locked in the breasts of solitary thinkers, and hidden among Latin folios—burst forth like a conqueror upon the world they were destined to transform, under the title of the Rights of Man.[5]

Natural rights are the rights that individuals possess in a state of nature, before creating governments. In a society with no government, individuals possess complete autonomy, which is bounded only by the equal autonomy possessed by other individuals. The fact that the boundaries of rights are not clear leads to the "law of nature" as defined by John Locke: "no one ought to harm another in his life, health, liberty, or possessions."[6] Only by respecting this unwritten law could individuals expect their own rights would be respected in turn.

Natural rights, then, are very broad and subject to few constraints; but they are also very insecure, as anyone asserting force can invade the rights of others. For that reason, individuals form governments to secure their rights. They create "social contracts," surrendering to government a small part of their autonomy in exchange for greater protection of the remaining rights. The United States Constitution is such a social contract.

Though many of the key architects of the American revolution, including Thomas Jefferson, Patrick Henry, George Mason, Benjamin

*The term "classical liberalism" refers to the broader philosophy of natural rights reflected in the American civil rights vision.

Franklin, and others embraced the philosophy of natural rights, it appears that the first to define the concept of "civil rights" was Thomas Paine. For Paine, a "civil right" is "a natural right exchanged" by individuals entering society on creation of a social contract. As Paine explained,

> Man did not enter into society to . . . have less rights than he had before, but to have those rights better secured. . . . Every civil right has for its foundation some natural right pre-existing in the individual, but to which his individual power is not, in all cases, sufficiently competent.[7]

The purpose of government, its raison d'être, is to secure those civil rights. Government's power inherently is limited to those powers expressly delegated by the people for the purpose of more effectively securing their civil rights, and the people cannot cede to government power over others that they do not themselves possess. Hence, the legitimate power of government is extremely narrow, and the civil rights retained by individuals remain inviolable.

In addition to the concept of inalienable civil rights, Paine contributed to the American civil rights vision the corollary principle of equality of rights. "Whenever I use the words *freedom* or *rights*," declared Paine, "I desire to mean an absolute equality of them. . . . It is this broad base, this universal foundation, that gives security to all and every part of society."[8] The principle of equality of rights is "clear and simple," Paine explained, for "where the rights of man are equal, every man must finally see the necessity of protecting the rights of others as the most effectual security for his own."[9] Paine displayed remarkable prescience when he warned that whenever we

> depart from the principle of equal rights, or attempt any modification of it, we plunge into a labyrinth of difficulties from which there is no way out but by retreating. Where are we to stop? Or by what principle are we to find out the point to stop at, that shall discriminate between men of the same country, part of whom shall be free, and the rest not?[10]

The belief that equality of rights may be compromised, observed Paine, "has already been fatal to thousands, who, not contented with *equal rights*, have sought more till they lost all, and experienced in themselves the degrading *inequality* they endeavored to fix upon others."[11]

From the outset, those who believed in civil rights recognized that while the state was necessary to secure civil rights through enforcement of a rule of law, the state also was the greatest threat to civil rights. For if the state enjoys a monopoly over the legal use of coercion and physical force, it also therefore has a tremendous propensity for abuse. Hence the architects of civil rights were keen to stress that the protection of civil rights ultimately is government's primary role, and that government possesses only those powers explicitly ceded to it by the people. Moreover, the state itself must scrupulously adhere to the rule of law.

This tension between the state as a *guarantor* of civil rights and a *violator* of civil rights is an issue recurrent throughout the quest for civil rights in America. By and large, until recent years, the principal task of the civil rights movement has been to restrict the power of government. Indeed, the defining difference between the civil rights establishment of the past 30 years and its predecessors is the recent tendency to employ the state's coercive arsenal against private individuals, rather than to restrain the state's power to violate civil rights, a phenomenon explored in greater detail in the next chapter.

In any event, the civil rights vision constructed on the principles of natural rights was incorporated into the nation's founding charters. The vision gained its ultimate expression in the Declaration of Independence, which proclaimed the "self-evident" principles that "all men are created equal" and "endowed by their Creator with certain unalienable Rights," among which are "Life, Liberty and the pursuit of Happiness." In order "to secure these rights, Governments are instituted among Men, deriving their just powers from the consent of the governed."

The Constitution also was built upon natural rights principles. The preamble speaks of establishing a social contract:

> We the People of the United States, in Order to form a more perfect Union, establish Justice, insure domestic Tranquility, provide for the common defence, promote the general Welfare, and secure the Blessings of Liberty to ourselves and our Posterity, do ordain and establish this Constitution for the United States of America.

Likewise, the Bill of Rights, particularly the Ninth and Tenth Amendments, sought to preserve the maximum possible sphere of individual autonomy and to make clear that the new government possessed

27

only those powers explicitly delegated to it.[12] The Ninth Amendment provides,

> The enumeration in the Constitution, of certain rights, shall not be construed to deny or disparage others retained by the people.

The Tenth Amendment states,

> The powers not delegated to the United States by the Constitution, nor prohibited by it to the States, are reserved to the States respectively, or to the people.

Together, these provisions establish that the primary purpose of government is to protect individual rights, even against democratic majorities. Paine and others referred to this vision as our "first principles," which have informed the American civil rights vision from its beginnings, and against which we ought measure progress even today.

But the same Constitution that served as a charter of civil rights also embodied a blatant nullification of civil rights: the institution of human slavery. Slavery was present in America long before the civil rights vision that eventually would bring about its demise. And unquestionably, slavery was incompatible with natural rights principles. As Sir William Blackstone observed in his *Commentaries on the Law of England*, slavery is an affront to freedom of contract, which is the cornerstone of a free society, for "what equivalent can be given for life and liberty, both of which, in absolute slavery, are held to be in the master's disposal?"[13]

Yet many of the architects of the American republic were themselves slaveholders, and the institution received tacit approval in the Constitution, which in Article 1, Section 2 counted a slave as three-fifths of a man for purposes of apportioning congressional representation; and in Article 1, Section 9 prohibited Congress from prohibiting the slave trade until 1808. This fundamental conflict between ideals and practices—a conflict that has recurred in various forms throughout American history—gave rise to the first organized civil rights movement in America, the abolitionists. Their goal, shared with all other civil rights movements during the nation's first two centuries, was to reconcile American practices with American ideals.

The first American abolitionists were the Pennsylvania Quakers, who declared in 1688 that slavery was incompatible with the rights of free people: "Here is liberty of conscience, which is right and reasonable; here ought to be likewise liberty of body."[14] Slaves themselves believed that the republic's founding ideals spoke directly to their condition, as reflected by a petition for freedom submitted during the American Revolution: "Every principle from which America has acted in the course of her difficulties with Great-Britain, pleads stronger than a thousand arguments for your Petitioners."[15] Several revolutionary leaders, including John Adams and Thomas Jefferson, argued without success for an explicit repudiation of slavery in the Declaration of Independence; and others such as Paine, John Jay, Benjamin Franklin, and Alexander Hamilton were active abolitionists.[16]

But with the accommodation with slavery made in the Constitution, the task of abolition fell largely to a later group of revolutionaries, who again drew from natural rights philosophy for their moral vision.

Nineteenth century abolitionists differed in their tactics. Some focused on "manumission," that is, purchasing the freedom of individual slaves. Others focused on outright abolition. Some believed that the Constitution, properly construed, forbade slavery, while others were convinced that constitutional change was necessary to bring practice into harmony with principle.[17]

Among the abolitionists who believed radical change was necessary was William Lloyd Garrison. He launched his abolitionist crusade, which would last nearly 35 years, with the antislavery publication *The Liberator*. Its first issue in 1831 captured the movement's urgency and moral certainty:

> I will be harsh as truth, and as uncompromising as justice. On this subject, I do not wish to think, or speak, or write with moderation. No! No! Tell a man whose house is on fire to give a moderate alarm; tell him to moderately rescue his wife from the hands of the ravisher; ... but urge me not to use moderation in a cause like the present. I am in earnest—I will not equivocate—I will not excuse—I will not retreat a single inch—AND I WILL BE HEARD.[18]

The abolitionists consistently sounded natural rights principles, presenting a clear civil rights vision. Foremost among them was Frederick Douglass, a runaway slave and later a freeman who became a publisher and public speaker in the cause of abolition. In 1849 he declared,

> It is evident that white and black "must fall or flourish together." In the light of this great truth, laws ought to be enacted, and institutions established—all distinctions, founded on complexion, ought to be repealed, repudiated, and forever abolished—and every right, privilege, and immunity, now enjoyed by the white man, ought to be as freely granted to the man of color.[19]

Another great abolitionist was Charles Sumner, a lawyer who later would be elected to the U.S. Senate and play a leading role in the post-Civil War constitutional amendments. Expounding natural rights principles, Sumner in 1849 urged the Massachusetts Supreme Court to strike down school segregation:

> The equality which was declared by our fathers in 1776 . . . was equality before the law. Its object was to efface all political or civil distinctions. . . . This is the Great Charter of every person who draws his vital breath upon this soil. . . . [H]e is a MAN—the equal of all his fellow-men.[20]

Although the court rejected Sumner's argument, the abolitionists finally convinced the Massachusetts legislature to open the public schools on an equal basis in 1855.[21]

Despite constant efforts, the abolitionist movement suffered severe setbacks in the 1850s. The Fugitive Slave Law, enacted in 1850, denied runaway slaves the basic due process rights to testify or receive a jury trial, while presuming their guilt. In 1857, the Supreme Court officially relegated blacks to an inferior status, ruling in its infamous *Dred Scott* decision that emancipated blacks could not sue in the courts because they could not be members of the political community.[22] Looking back to the American founding, Chief Justice Roger Taney concluded that blacks

> were at that time considered as a subordinate and inferior class of beings, who had been subjugated by the dominant race, and whether emancipated or not, yet remained subject to their authority, and had no rights or privileges but such as those who held the power and the government might choose to grant them.[23]

This decision nullified the natural rights of black individuals, and made clear that nothing less than sweeping constitutional revision would fulfill America's promise of civil rights.

The *Dred Scott* decision and preceding events unified the abolitionists, who came together in the newly created Republican Party, which nominated Abraham Lincoln for president in 1860. Lincoln asserted that equality was the defining characteristic of republican government, and that "[t]he entire records of the world . . . may be searched in vain for one single affirmation . . . that the negro was not included in the Declaration of Independence." The institution of slavery, he lamented, "forces so many really good people amongst ourselves into an open war with the very fundamental principles of civil liberty."[24]

While for Lincoln the purpose of the ensuing Civil War was to preserve the republic, for the abolitionists it was a moral crusade to end slavery and establish civil rights. Following the Civil War, the abolitionists exerted powerful influence in Congress through the so-called "radical" Republicans. Never before or since has a Congress been so motivated by philosophical absolutes; nor in a position (with southern Democrats largely absent) to so completely implement their agenda.

Their ire was fueled in the aftermath of the war by the actions of recalcitrant southern legislatures to keep the newly emancipated blacks in a state of subservience. The chosen vehicle was the "black codes": laws designed to nullify such economic liberties as freedom of labor, contract, and property ownership. Congress responded by passing the Civil Rights Act of 1866, which protected the rights of contract and property ownership and guaranteed the "full and equal benefit of all laws [for] the security of persons and property."

President Andrew Johnson vetoed the law, contending it was beyond Congress's power to enact, and Congress overrode his veto. But the radical Republicans, chastened by past experiences with a hostile Supreme Court and inadequate constitutional protections for individual rights, decided to "constitutionalize" the Civil Rights Act of 1866. In addition to passing the Thirteenth Amendment prohibiting involuntary servitude and the Fifteenth Amendment protecting federal voting rights, it enacted the Fourteenth Amendment, the main provisions of which establish that

> No State shall make or enforce any law which shall abridge the privileges or immunities of citizens of the United States; nor shall any State deprive any person of life, liberty, or property, without due process of law; nor deny to any person within its jurisdiction the equal protection of the laws.

31

The amendment was aimed at restricting the power of state governments, which were the principal violators of civil rights; and at protecting the civil and economic liberties contained in the Bill of Rights and the Civil Rights Act of 1866 within the ambit of the "privileges or immunities" of citizens.

But barely was the ink dry on the Fourteenth Amendment when the Supreme Court eviscerated the privileges or immunities clause in the aptly named *Slaughter-House Cases* in 1872.[25] The case was brought by a group of butchers who argued that the creation by the State of Louisiana of a cattle slaughterhouse monopoly that destroyed the butchers' livelihoods violated their economic liberty protected by the privileges or immunities clause. By a 5–4 vote—exceedingly rare in those days—the Supreme Court ruled against the butchers, contending quite remarkably that the privileges or immunities clause did not add to the substantive rights protected against state infringement. Since 1872, although the due process and equal protection clauses of the Fourteenth Amendment have repeatedly been invoked to strike down state laws, the privileges or immunities clause has almost never been applied to limit the power of state governments, no matter how oppressive.[26]

*Slaughter-House* unleashed southern state governments to replace slavery with apartheid. So-called "Jim Crow" laws imposed not only social segregation, but barriers to voting rights (such as poll taxes and literacy tests) and to economic liberties. In sum, the laws were intended to keep blacks segregated, politically powerless, and economically servile. The 1896 Supreme Court ruling in *Plessy v. Ferguson*, upholding the "separate but equal" doctrine, gave virtual carte blanche to the Jim Crow regime.

Ironically, the roots of *Plessy* lay in *Slaughter-House*. *Plessy* was a test case supported by private railroad companies who for economic reasons wanted to overturn the ban on integrated transit. The plaintiff, Homer Plessy, was one-eighth black, but was denied a seat in a first-class car because he was considered black under Louisiana law. The most straightforward argument—that Plessy was denied freedom of contract—was no longer possible because of the evisceration of economic liberties in *Slaughter-House*. So he had to make the argument—historically more difficult—that the Fourteenth Amendment's equal protection clause forbade racial segregation.[27] The Court disagreed, ruling that race-based distinctions are valid if they are "reasonable," and "with respect to this there must necessarily be a large discretion on the part of the legislature."[28]

In dissent, Justice John Harlan gave lone voice to the American civil rights vision. For Harlan, the statute plainly was "inconsistent with the personal liberty of citizens, white and black," and the Court's decision made a mockery of the "recent amendments of the supreme law, which established universal civil freedom, ... obliterated the race line from our systems of governments, national and state, and placed our free institutions upon the broad and sure foundation of the equality of all men before the law."[29] He declared,

> [I]n view of the Constitution, in the eye of the law, there is in this country no superior, dominant, ruling class of citizens. There is no caste here. Our Constitution is color-blind, and neither knows nor tolerates classes among citizens. In respect of civil rights, all citizens are equal before the law. The humblest is the peer of the most powerful. The law regards man as man, and takes no account of his surroundings or of his color when his civil rights as guaranteed by the supreme law of the land are involved. It is therefore to be regretted that this high tribunal, the final expositor of the fundamental law of the land, has reached the conclusion that it is competent for a state to regulate the enjoyment by citizens of their civil rights solely on the basis of race.[30]

*Plessy* marked a crucial and disastrous turning point, away from principles of civil rights and in favor of a regime in which fundamental rights were subordinated to racist social engineering. For the advocates of the American civil rights vision, those were dark days.

Two strategies were put forward to effect positive change. One was the philosophy of self-help championed by Booker T. Washington, who urged blacks to develop their skills. Washington's philosophy was expressed in 1901 by a black congressman, Rep. George C. White:

> I want to submit a brief recipe for the solution of the so-called American negro problem. He asks no special favors, but simply demands that he be given the same chance for existence, for earning a livelihood, for raising himself in the scales of manhood and womanhood that are accorded to kindred nationalities.[31]

Washington's strategy was remarkably successful given the massive Jim Crow economic restraints,[32] but over time it gave way to the strategy that would dominate the quest for civil rights for the next century: political and legal action. Much has been made of the differences between Booker T. Washington and W.E.B. DuBois, who urged the new approach, but in terms of principles and ultimate objectives the two movements were complementary. "There are to-day no truer exponents of the pure human spirit of the Declaration of Independence than the American Negroes," declared DuBois in his 1903 manifesto, *The Souls of Black Folk*.[33]

The political campaign found its vehicle with the creation of the NAACP in 1909. The rationale, remarked Oswald Garrison Villard, one of its founders, was that the race problem "will not work itself out by the mere lapse of time or by the operation of education. There is only one remedy—that the colored people shall have every one of the privileges and rights of American citizens."[34] The NAACP committed itself to "the abolition of color-hyphenation and the substitution of straight Americanism," through equal voting rights, equal educational opportunity, fair trials, the right to sit on juries, anti-lynching laws, equal access to public services, and equal employment opportunities.[35] These goals would form the central focus in the quest for civil rights for the next 45 years.

Since voting rights were suppressed and political action was unlikely to succeed, much of the effort during that period was directed toward the courts. The judicial branch was designed by the framers as an independent body whose members are appointed for life, and whose purpose is to ensure that the legislative and executive branches (and, by virtue of the Fourteenth Amendment, the states) do not stray beyond their constitutional powers. The judiciary is the ultimate guardian of individual rights.[36] The NAACP's legal strategy involved a series of cases designed to build not only legal precedents but public support, until the edifice of *Plessy v. Ferguson* came tumbling down.[37]

There were some serious setbacks along the way. Among the most pernicious was the internment of Japanese-Americans during World War II, which was upheld as an emergency military measure by the United States Supreme Court in its 1944 decision in *Korematsu v. United States*. In dissent, Justice Robert Jackson reasserted the principle of equality under law:

> [A] judicial construction . . . that will sustain this order is a far more subtle blow to liberty than the promulgation of the order itself. . . .

[O]nce a judicial opinion rationalizes the Constitution to show that
[it] sanctions such an order ... the Court for all time has validated
the principle of racial discrimination. ... The principle then lies about
like a loaded weapon ready for the hand of any authority that can
bring forward a plausible claim of an urgent need.[38]

Yet World War II was a turning point for civil rights. Hitler's
totalitarian regime rested on an ideology of racial purity, a concept
that offended American sensibilities, even as the United States main-
tained a sordid record of its own. Black Americans fought bravely
for their country—yet they returned to segregation and second-class
citizenship. The war forced Americans to face the inconsistency
between their principles and their practices.

It was in this period of critical self-examination that the modern
civil rights movement was born. Though the period from 1945
through 1965 often has been characterized as a civil rights "revolution"—and indeed systemic social change occurred—the civil rights
movement by contrast fundamentally was conservative. Its roots lay
in the soil of religion and American democracy. It did not question
American values and principles, but embraced them. "The rhetoric
of freedom permeated the movement from the beginning," observes
historian Richard H. King.[39] The movement anchored its cause firmly
in what Gunnar Myrdal, in his 1944 study, *An American Dilemma,*
described as the "American Creed": the "ideals of the essential
dignity of the individual human being, of the fundamental equality
of all men, and of certain inalienable rights to freedom, justice, and
a fair opportunity."[40] As Paul M. Sniderman and Thomas Piazza
observe in their recent book, *The Scar of Race,* Myrdal believed that
the American Creed was "the highest card to be played in the politics
of civil rights, the one that would trump all the others." The attach-
ment of civil rights to the American Creed "elevated the issue of
race onto a different plane and made it so quintessentially a moral
issue. Civil rights was not pork barrel politics: it was not just an
effort to make blacks better off, but a larger crusade in behalf of
what Americans, white as well as black, agreed is just."[41]

The union activist A. Philip Randolph drew on those principles
in a mass march on Washington in 1941 protesting policies toward
blacks. He demanded "the abrogation of every law which makes a
distinction in treatment between citizens based on religion, creed,
color, or national origin."[42] After World War II, President Harry

Truman named a Committee on Civil Rights, declaring that the "immediate task is to remove the last remnants of the barriers which stand between millions of our citizens and their birthright."[43] The Committee's report, entitled *To Secure These Rights*, called for action to curb violations of four essential rights: the right to safety and security, to citizenship and its privileges, to freedom of conscience and expression, and to equality of opportunity.[44]

A series of legal challenges to segregation led to the 1954 decision in *Brown v. Board of Education* that struck down segregated schools as a violation of the Fourteenth Amendment's guarantee of equality under law.[45] Arguing for the NAACP, Thurgood Marshall framed the terms of the debate by invoking the American civil rights vision:

> The importance to our American democracy of the substantive question can hardly be overstated. The question is whether a nation founded on the proposition that "all men are created equal" is honoring its commitments to grant "due process of law" and "the equal protection of the laws" . . . when it, or one of its constituent states, confers or denies benefits on the basis of color or race.[46]

The NAACP's brief traced the evolution of civil rights from their origins in natural rights as interpreted by John Locke and Thomas Jefferson through the ratification of the Fourteenth Amendment. The purpose of that amendment, the brief urged, was to "prohibit all state action predicated upon race or color." On this point Marshall was unequivocal: "That the Constitution is color blind is our dedicated belief."[47]

The legal triumphs paved the way for political action, the catalyst for which occurred when a black woman, Rosa Parks, refused to give up her seat on a segregated bus in Montgomery, Alabama. The incident sparked a boycott led by a young black minister, the Rev. Martin Luther King Jr. For King, Parks symbolized far more than a tired woman engaged in an act of momentary protest: "She was anchored to that seat by the accumulated indignities of days gone by and the boundless aspirations of generations yet unborn."[48]

What helped make King so successful was that he, like the great civil rights leaders before him, rooted his campaign in the American civil rights vision, invoking time and again the natural rights principles upon which the nation was founded.[49] He asked not for special treatment or retribution, but only for the basic rights and opportunities that all Americans cherish. "Our goal is freedom," he declared.

"I believe we will win it because the goal of the nation is freedom."[50] Emphatically, he clasped as well the universality of rights. To whites, King declared: "One day we shall win freedom, but not only for ourselves. We shall so appeal to your heart and conscience that we shall win *you* in the process, and our victory will be a double victory."[51]

For King, the Declaration of Independence was the highest expression of the civil rights vision, what King described as the "American dream." His analysis of the essential elements of this vision—inalienable rights held by all in equal measure—was keen. "One of the first things we notice in this dream," King remarked, "is an amazing universalism. It does not say some men, but it says all men." And what "ultimately distinguishes . . . our form of government from all of the totalitarian regimes that emerge in history," said King, is that our system "says that each individual has certain basic rights that are neither conferred by nor derived from the state."[52] In his "I Have a Dream" speech on the steps of the Lincoln Memorial in 1963, King defined those rights:

> When the architects of our republic wrote the magnificent words of the Constitution and the Declaration of Independence, they were signing a promissory note to which every American would fall heir. This note was a promise that all men, yes, black men as well as white men, would be guaranteed the unalienable rights of life, liberty, and the pursuit of happiness.[53]

Despite the clear articulation of this classical liberal view of civil rights, the movement during the 1960s subtly embraced a change in goals: it sought not merely to curb government's power to violate civil rights, which was the movement's preeminent objective through *Brown v. Board of Education*, but to use government's power to eliminate racism and restrict individual freedom of association. Though seemingly beneficent and couched in much the same rhetoric, this shift in the movement's goals presaged a massive expansion of government power, which I shall explore in subsequent chapters.

Still, what is striking about this brief recounting of the history of the quest for civil rights is the remarkable consistency and continuity of the underlying classical liberal vision. The essential themes of universalism, equality under law, colorblindness, and basic individual rights are sounded time and again. If one took the great civil rights leaders at different periods of American history—whether

Tom Paine, or William Lloyd Garrison, or Frederick Douglass, or Booker T. Washington, or W. E. B. DuBois, or Martin Luther King Jr.—and randomly arranged their descriptions of their civil rights visions, it would be difficult for even the most accomplished of historians to distinguish among them.

What is also remarkable is that the great triumphs in the quest for civil rights—the abolition of slavery, the constitutional guarantee of equal protection, the repudiation of Jim Crow—all were informed by this vision. America's success or lack thereof in fulfilling its moral commitment to civil rights can be measured by its adherence to the classical liberal vision: when the nation has acted in accordance with the underlying natural rights principles, it has succeeded; when it has strayed from those principles, we find ourselves moving backwards.

As we confront the dilemmas described in the pages that follow, we would do well to consult the lessons of history and to rediscover the principles underlying the quest for civil rights, of which recently we seem tragically to have lost sight. If we do, perhaps we can rekindle the dream so eloquently described by Martin Luther King Jr.:

> A dream of equality of opportunity, of privilege and property widely distributed; a dream of a land where men no longer argue that the color of a man's skin determines the content of his character; the dream of a land where every man will respect the dignity and worth of human personality—this is the dream. When it is realized, the jangling discords of our nation will be transformed into a beautiful symphony of brotherhood, and men everywhere will know that America is truly the land of the free and the home of the brave.[54]

# 3. The Revised Agenda

You guys have been practicing discrimination for years. Now it is our turn.

—Justice Thurgood Marshall[1]

To ignore race and sex is racist and sexist.

—Jesse Jackson[2]

In nearly every discussion about civil rights and race relations, the same question arises: given what we thought we accomplished in the 1960s, how did we end up where we are today?[3]

Like many people who puzzle over this question, I am too young to remember much about the civil rights struggles of the 1960s. Images at the periphery of my childhood memories reflect a time of violent riots, mass demonstrations, tension, and upheaval. And yet, to look at that period from the vantage point of history, there must have been for the participants in the civil rights movement a heady feeling of unparalleled excitement and triumph. For after two centuries, our nation seemed finally on the verge of delivering on its most sacred promises of basic rights and equal opportunities for all Americans. It was a time of tremendous hope, for racial healing and harmony, for tangible progress on both social and economic fronts.

Such hopes necessarily would be tempered by grim realities. No one expected the transition from segregation to equal opportunity to be easy, or the people who were infected with racism suddenly to realize the error of their ways or easily surrender the reins of power. But one thing seemed clear: the civil rights movement was determined to end once and for all government's power to classify Americans on the basis of race.

Given that fact, who possibly could have predicted the race-consciousness that permeates the American landscape 30 years later?

Who could have imagined that laws designed to eradicate discrimination could be interpreted to permit or require discrimination? Who could have conceived of the regime of classifications that apportions opportunities in education, employment, and voting on the basis of race and gender? Who would have been so pessimistic as to project the growth of a massive underclass that has benefitted hardly at all from the accomplishments of the civil rights revolution?

The explanation lies in the radically changed goals and philosophy of the civil rights movement after 1954. Until then, the movement's goals had been to increase individual autonomy and to limit the power of government to infringe on civil rights. Those who wanted to deny rights to blacks or other minorities often had turned to the state to enforce racial predilections that could not be sustained in a free society, whether legal support for slavery, suppression of freedom of contract, or enforcement of segregation.

Indeed, before 1964, the movement's leaders seemed to acknowledge that the power of government to regulate individual thoughts and to restrict freedom of association was both dangerous and ineffectual. As Martin Luther King Jr. declared in a 1962 speech before a church conference in Nashville:

> I can summarize all that I have been saying by affirming that the demands of desegregation are enforceable demands while the demands of integration fall within the scope of unenforceable demands. . . . The former are regulated by codes of society and the vigorous implementation of law-enforcement agencies. . . . But unenforceable obligations are beyond the reach of the laws of society. . . . A vigorous enforcement of civil rights laws will bring an end to segregated public facilities which are barriers to a truly desegregated society, but it cannot bring an end to fears, prejudice, pride, and irrationality, which are the barriers to a truly integrated society.[4]

But in the early 1960s, the movement began to move beyond its traditional aims to embrace regulation of private actions. Though subtle, the obliteration of the distinction between the public and private spheres would provide the foundation for all the mischief that would follow in the name of civil rights.

The shift was subtle and appeared beneficent. President John F. Kennedy responded to King's 1963 Lincoln Memorial address by calling upon Congress "to make a commitment it has not fully made in this century to the proposition that race has no place in American life or law."[5] Removing race-consciousness from the realm of law was, of course, a prime objective of the civil rights law. And eliminating racism from society was certainly one of the movement's key moral objectives. But using the coercive power of government to regulate private attitudes and actions—precisely what King emphasized was beyond the realm of government—constituted a major departure from the movement's traditional objectives.

But that was the issue presented by the proposed Civil Rights Act of 1964. The act entrusted to the federal government the awesome power to prevent individuals from discriminating in employment and public accommodations and to punish them for doing so. This task requires the state to police the private thoughts and motivations of individuals, an inherently dangerous power that, once conferred, is difficult to constrain.

Every restraint against discrimination interferes with freedom of association and reduces the choices individuals otherwise are free to make. As University of Chicago law professor Richard Epstein argues, "An antidiscrimination law is the antithesis of freedom of contract, a principle that allows all persons to do business with whomever they please for good reason, bad reason, or no reason at all."[6]

These concerns were raised in the course of the debates over the Civil Rights Act. The law sparked fierce opposition, not only on reactionary grounds of racism and states' rights, but on libertarian grounds of concern for individual autonomy. Whenever "the morals of the majority are self-righteously imposed upon a minority," argued Robert H. Bork in 1963, the "discussion we ought to hear is of the cost in freedom that must be paid for such legislation, the morality of enforcing morals through law, and the likely consequences for law enforcement of trying to do so." Bork declared,

> The principle of such legislation is that if I find your behavior ugly by my standards, moral or aesthetic, and if you prove stubborn about adopting my view of the situation, I am justified in having the state coerce you into more righteous paths. That is itself a principle of unsurpassed ugliness.[7]

In a free society, restraints on freedom of association and contract are justifiable only to prevent violations against the rights of others. Freedom of contract, for instance, does not encompass the power to enslave another. But the civil rights laws went beyond restraints against coercion to tread directly upon voluntary freedom of association among private individuals. To this extent the laws contradicted the civil rights movement's classical liberal tradition, which places paramount value upon individual sovereignty.

If there was any counterbalance to the risk of expanding government power, at least it appeared that the regime of official discriminatory policies was coming to an end. Even Richard Epstein, a leading modern critic of the Civil Rights Act, acknowledges,

> So great were the abuses of political power before 1964 that, knowing what I know today, if given an all-or-nothing choice, I should still have voted in favor of the Civil Rights Act in order to allow federal power to break the stranglehold of local government on race relations.[8]

Moreover, the architects of the Civil Rights Act responded to libertarian concerns by emphasizing that the interference with private autonomy was slight and in accord with widely shared principles of fairness. The law would ensure that in the areas of employment, education, and public accommodations, people would be judged as individuals without regard to their race, color, national origin, religion, or sex.

More than anything else, the law was aimed at removing race as a decisionmaking criterion in public life. On this point the act's framers could not have been more emphatic. The aim of the civil rights law, as one Senate sponsor described it, was to produce a society in which "the color of a man's skin . . . [is] completely extraneous."[9] Another sponsor declared that "the bill . . . is colorblind."[10] The lead sponsor, Sen. Hubert H. Humphrey, explained that

> our standard of judgment in the last analysis is not some group's power . . . but an *equal* opportunity for *persons*.
>
> Do you want a society that is nothing but an endless power struggle among organized groups? Do you want a society where there is no place for the independent individual? I don't.[11]

But no matter how modest the law's objectives, the Civil Rights Act of 1964 clearly sanctioned an unprecedented intrusion into individual autonomy. No meaningful restraints existed to prevent future expansions of government power. Perhaps predictably, in every area covered by federal civil rights statutes, the powers have expanded even as the "emergency" justifications have receded.

Perhaps nothing reflects the chasm between the law's stated objectives and the reality of its evolution than the changed rhetoric of civil rights. Unlike their predecessors, today's self-proclaimed civil rights leaders no longer quote from the Declaration of Independence. They speak not about individuals but groups, not about liberty but entitlements, not about opportunity but outcomes, not about colorblindness but preferential treatment. The conceptual metamorphosis is precisely 180 degrees: in today's debate, to be in favor of nondiscrimination is to be castigated as anti-civil rights.

The changed rhetoric reflects a fundamental transformation in the philosophy of civil rights that built on the expanded power of government created by the Civil Rights Act of 1964 and subsequent enactments. What evolved over the course of the 1960s was a radical revised agenda that would come to completely supplant the traditional civil rights vision.[12] Every basic precept of the vision was jettisoned.

A few years ago, I noted this phenomenon to a very liberal friend of mine who was an active participant in the civil rights struggles of the 1960s. Why, I asked him, did the movement abandon the principles it had so consistently invoked, after the revolution succeeded? He smiled and replied, "We abandoned those principles because we never really believed in them."

I hope there is much more to the phenomenon than that; and yet I think there is an element of truth to it. The civil rights movement in the 1960s did not operate in a vacuum. Despite the vindication of traditional civil rights principles, America was in no mood to celebrate. The nation was engulfed in a debilitating convulsion of cynicism and despair, fueled by the escalating war in Vietnam and the assassinations of John F. Kennedy and, later, of Martin Luther King Jr. America was seriously questioning its fundamental ideals, the very ideals that formed the foundation of the civil rights vision.

Like other political movements operating in the mid-'60s and beyond, the civil rights movement was heavily influenced by intellectual forces that were hostile to traditional American values and principles. One of the leading thinkers of this period was Michael Harrington, who in 1963 published a book called *The Other America*, which provided the intellectual foundation for President Lyndon

Johnson's "Great Society" welfare programs. Harrington depicted America's "affluent society" as enjoying the "highest standard of life the world has ever known," yet having within it "a culture of poverty" that is "beyond progress, sunk in a paralyzing, maiming routine."[13] The poor, Harrington asserted, "are so submerged in their poverty that one cannot begin to think about free choice."[14] Therefore, securing equal opportunity was not enough, Harrington concluded. "There is only one institution capable of acting to abolish poverty. That is the Federal Government."[15]

Echoing Harrington's analysis was Christopher Jencks, who eschewed traditional mechanisms for upward mobility such as education, in favor of government paternalism. "We need to establish the idea that the federal government is responsible not only for the total amount of the national income," Jencks proclaimed, "but for its distribution."[16]

These themes were embraced by the civil rights leadership, which was trying to come to grips with the widespread disillusionment among many blacks over the lack of tangible economic gains following the civil rights revolution. As King remarked in a 1966 television interview, "I think the real problem today is there is still a tragic gulf between promise and fulfillment, and that the rising expectations of freedom and equality, the rising expectations of improvement have met with little results."[17]

These impulses were fueled by the growing influence of black separatists such as Malcolm X and Stokely Carmichael. The separatists' appeal was explicitly racial: as Malcolm X exhorted his followers, "[W]e all have in common the greatest binding tie we could have ... we all are *black* people. ... Our enemy is the *white man!*"[18] Carmichael's radical platform called for "reallocation of land, of money."[19]

During that period, as historian James M. Washington observes, "it seemed that the civil rights leadership was being bypassed by the new advocates of black power."[20] This led King and other mainstream civil rights leaders to move left and embrace an ambitious social agenda. As activist Bayard Rustin observed, the "civil rights movement is evolving from a protest movement into a full-fledged *social movement*—an evolution calling its very name into question."[21] Where the civil rights movement traditionally had disdained the power of the state except as guardian of essential liberties, it now looked to the state to redistribute wealth. Whitney Young, for instance, demanded "family allowances ... *as a matter of right,*" guaranteed minimum incomes as a "*right* to which people are entitled," and "every family's *right* to a decent home."[22] King likewise called for a national guaranteed income, but acknowledged, "This proposal is not a 'civil rights' program, in the sense that that term is currently used."[23]

This new emphasis entailed a shift in the movement's objectives, substituting the emphasis on liberty that had propelled the movement for 200 years with a demand for equal outcomes.[24] It also presaged a change in the movement's tactics. "How are these radical objectives to be achieved?" asked Bayard Rustin. "The answer is simple, deceptively so—*through political power.*"[25] For the first time, the civil rights movement determined to use the power of government not to secure basic rights but to redistribute wealth and opportunities.

But along what lines? Though proceeding in tandem with the so-called war on poverty, the civil rights movement called for delineations based on race. Morris Abram, a veteran of the civil rights movement, observes that during this period, the movement "turned away from its original principled campaign for equal justice under law to engage in an open contest for social and economic benefits conferred on the basis of race."[26] This forced the movement to renounce tacitly but completely core tenets it had held for more than 200 years: colorblindness and the universality of civil rights. These tenets were based on the belief that the only way to protect anyone's civil rights was to protect everyone's civil rights, and on the observation borne out by the constant lessons of history that government's power to discriminate is never benign.

Yet in the mid-1960s, the very people who fought so hard to secure equality under law were now persuaded that it was possible to constructively harness government's power to discriminate. The same Thurgood Marshall who had argued in *Brown v. Board of Education* that the Constitution was colorblind now voted consistently as a Supreme Court justice to sustain racial discrimination in favor of blacks. And the Civil Rights Act of 1964, a law whose architects had proclaimed it as colorblind, would be construed not only to permit certain forms of discrimination, but also to require it. Nowhere was that Orwellian sentiment put more bluntly than in Justice Harry

Blackmun's remark in the 1978 *Regents of the University of California v. Bakke*: "In order to get beyond racism, we must first take account of race. . . . And in order to treat some persons equally, we must treat them differently."[27]

Effectuating racial redistribution required two additional changes to the civil rights vision: a definition of civil rights as inhering in groups rather than individuals, and a definition of equality to encompass outcomes rather than opportunity. Since civil rights deprivations had been inflicted on the basis of race, the movement's leaders reasoned, it is appropriate that remedies be conferred in the same fashion. Bayard Rustin identified this as the defining distinction between the modern civil rights movement and its "classical" antecedents: the "victory of the concept of collective struggle over individual achievement as the road to Negro freedom."[28]

The revised agenda was previewed by President Johnson in a 1965 speech at Howard University, when he stated that "we seek not just . . . equality as a right and a theory but equality as a fact and as a result."[29] With this pronouncement, observes Glenn Loury, "a very powerful idea was born"—"the general presumption that, due to our history of social oppression, blacks' failure to reach parity in American society derives exclusively from the effects of past and ongoing racism, and can only be remedied through state intervention."[30] Jesse Jackson put it simply: "Equality can be measured," he declared. "It can be turned into numbers."[31] Thus the practice of counting by race was reborn.

The revised agenda constituted a sweeping departure from the consensus on which the Civil Rights Act of 1964 was constructed. As Nathan Glazer describes it,

> In 1964, we declared that no account should be taken of race, color, national origin, or religion in the spheres of voting, jobs, and education. . . . Yet no sooner had we made this national assertion than we entered into an unexampled recording of the records of the color, race, and national origin in every significant sphere of [a person's] life. Having placed into law the dissenting opinion of *Plessy v. Ferguson* that our Constitution is color-blind, we entered into a period of color and group-consciousness with a vengeance.[32]

How could the civil rights leaders so brazenly jettison their core beliefs without someone calling them to account? One reason is the guilt the civil rights movement assigned to white Americans, which

stifled dissent. Author Charles Silberman gave voice to this sentiment in 1962 when he decried the "sins for which all Americans are
in some measure guilty and for which all Americans owe some act
of atonement."[33] This assignment of blame provided the foundation
for the regime of racial reparations that would follow.

Nathan Glazer identified a related part of the answer: the civil
rights leaders, he recognized, enjoyed an "enormous advantage.
They are seen as moral, and a moral advantage in politics, being on
the side of right, is worth a good deal."[34] Civil rights issues after
1964 would become an issue unique in American political discourse:
one over which a particular group of leaders, holding a well-defined
ideology and objectives, had an absolute, unquestioned moral
monopoly. Anyone who dared question their ideological orthodoxy
would be branded anti-civil rights or even racist.

This held true not only for those who had resisted the civil rights
revolution, but even for those who had been its allies. Martin Luther
King Jr. in 1967 complained that "when Negroes looked for . . . the
realization of equality, they found that many of their white allies had
quietly disappeared." The leader who once had spoken of universal
brotherhood, and who had forged biracial alliances based on shared
principles, now spoke with cynicism and bitterness:

> White America was ready to demand that the Negro should be
> spared the lash of brutality and coarse degradation, but it had never
> been truly committed to helping him out of poverty, exploitation
> or all forms of discrimination. The outraged white citizen had been
> sincere when he snatched the whips from the southern sheriffs and
> forbade them more cruelties. But when this was to a degree accom-
> plished, the emotions that had momentarily inflamed him melted
> away. White Americans left the Negro on the ground and in devastat-
> ing numbers walked off with the aggressor. It appeared that the
> white segregationist and the ordinary white citizen had more in
> common with one another than either had with the Negro.[35]

Accusations like these, even when rendered by those with far less
moral authority than King, would be leveled time and again, casting
moral condemnations upon dissenters and thereby neutralizing
opposition to whatever agenda the civil rights establishment cared
to assert. With King's death in 1968, the movement became progres-
sively less interested in staking its claims in the traditional civil
rights vision, or in seeking moral justifications for its positions. "I

don't think the movement as a whole has ever reclaimed its focus and its sense of moral authority and . . . moral leadership since the assassination of Martin Luther King Jr.,"[36] observes Rep. John Lewis (D-Ga.), a veteran of the civil rights movement.

Even without a moral compass, the burgeoning civil rights establishment grew to wield enormous influence in both the political and legal arenas. Civil rights groups teamed up with their former enemies, the labor unions, and with other liberal groups to form a powerful political alliance. In 1950, some of those divergent groups had formed the Leadership Conference on Civil Rights, which by the mid-1980s had grown to encompass 185 organizations, including the NAACP, American Civil Liberties Union, AFL-CIO, National Education Association, Anti-Defamation League of B'nai B'rith, National Organization for Women, American Association of Retired Persons, and People for the American Way.[37] The coalition's statement of purpose, fashioned to implement the recommendations of President Truman's civil rights commission, reflects the traditional civil rights vision: "We are committed to an integrated, democratic, plural society in which every individual is accorded equal rights, equal opportunities and equal justice without regard to race, sex, religion, ethnic origin, handicap or age," characteristics on which "there can be no distinctions."[38]

But by the 1960s, the entire civil rights establishment was pushing for racial quotas, forced busing, and proportional representation in the electoral arena. Recognizing that those goals diverged from the civil rights consensus and often could not be achieved through the democratic process, the civil rights establishment instead pressed much of its agenda through indirect political means: executive orders, bureaucratic regulations, and court decrees. The colorblind civil rights laws would provide the baseline from which the more ambitious race-conscious agenda would be pushed.

The civil rights establishment has exerted enormous influence in every administration, both Democrat and Republican. During the Carter administration, in particular, the two top civil rights officials, Assistant Attorney General for Civil Rights Drew Days and Equal Employment Opportunity Commission Chairperson Eleanor Holmes Norton, devoted their law enforcement arsenals to pursuit of the civil rights establishment's radical agenda.

The most fertile terrain on which to advance this agenda was the courts. Skilled legal advocates employed by such well-funded organizations as the NAACP Legal Defense and Educational Fund, Inc., and the Lawyers' Committee for Civil Rights adeptly used the courts to achieve what they could not hope to accomplish in the legislative arena.[39] Alumni of these organizations, such as Lani Guinier, Deval Patrick, and Norma Cantu, would go on to be nominated to top civil rights law enforcement positions in the Clinton administration (see Chapter 7).

The goal of this litigation program—whether directed toward housing, education, employment, or voting—was racial parity. In each of these areas, the civil rights litigators argued that deviations from statistical parity provided evidence of discrimination, and pushed for remedies to ensure proportionate outcomes. As the next three chapters will show, over a remarkably short period of time the concepts became deeply entrenched in all areas of civil rights law.

The net result of these concerted efforts in the political and legal arenas has been a profound transformation of the concept of civil rights. Equality of opportunity has been replaced by equality of results, colorblindness by race-consciousness, individual liberty by group reparations.

The revised agenda has dominated civil rights policies for 30 years, yet little effort has been made to evaluate its success or lack thereof. Indeed, any effort to do so is greeted with suspicion and hostility. Any failure to achieve the objective at the core of the agenda—racial parity—is deemed evidence of continuing racism, not of the inherently self-defeating nature of the agenda. Differences in individual talent, ambition, choices, experiences, and conditions of life are subsumed within notions of group identity and equal outcomes. Serious social problems that may contribute to unequal outcomes are swept under the carpet of racial redistribution, while backlash builds among those left out of the equation.

From a historical perspective, this should not come as a surprise. As a pragmatic matter, the new agenda was a desperate gamble. In a democracy it is always dangerous for minorities to demand special treatment, for such status depends on the tacit assent of the majority, which can withdraw it at will. Those who now decry the repeal of race-based "affirmative action" and other entitlements must always have been aware that appeals to white guilt would sustain special treatment for only so long—certainly for no longer than the last generation that had something about which to feel guilty.

Yet, if anything, the demand for racial reparations seems to grow more strident even as the basis for such reparations grows more attenuated. Among black Americans (including recent immigrants), fewer than half (about 45 percent) were born before the Civil Rights Act of 1964, and barely one in four (about 28 percent) were alive during the era of state-sanctioned segregation.[40] To the extent "temporary" departures from the principle of nondiscrimination are ever justified, such extraordinary measures would seem appropriately limited to those who suffered official discrimination during a time when the law provided no remedy—a time quickly receding into the distant past. Yet far from being phased out, race-based preferences continue to proliferate.

If American history has taught us anything at all, it is that government's awesome power to discriminate on the basis of immutable characteristics such as race or gender is inherently divisive and incendiary. Those who today claim the civil rights mantle did not learn that lesson. They thought the power to discriminate could be harnessed for beneficent purposes. They could not have been more gravely mistaken.

For 200 years, the civil rights movement set itself about the task of fulfilling a particular vision, defined by a coherent set of natural rights principles. There has been a nearly perfect correlation between principle and progress in the quest for civil rights: betrayal of the civil rights vision brought us slavery, Jim Crow, and internment camps; adherence to that vision brought us emancipation, the Fourteenth Amendment, and the promise of equal opportunity.

But now we are back to betraying the vision, and have been for the past 30 years. That betrayal has had real-world ramifications that touch the lives of every American. For as I shall demonstrate in the following chapters, "affirmative action" is more than reverse discrimination in jobs and educational opportunities: it is forced busing that has decimated inner-city public schools; it is racial gerrymandering that segregates voters by race; it is a pervasive race-consciousness that threatens to rend forever our social fabric. But most damaging of all is the erosion of a national consensus behind the American Creed—that set of agreed-upon values and principles that defines us as a nation and unites us as a people.

These are the terrible, if all too predictable, consequences of abandoning our civil rights vision.

# 4. Trickle-Down Civil Rights

It finally has come to this: racial preferences so permeate the American landscape that a supervisor can be punished by his public employer for *refusing* to discriminate.[1]

Dr. Stanley Dea comes from a family of Chinese immigrants who surmounted a history of discrimination to earn a share of the American dream as entrepreneurs and professionals. Through his own personal industry and talent, Dea rose to head the Washington Suburban Sanitary Commission's Bureau of Planning Design and to supervise a staff of 250 employees. Dea drew from those experiences an abiding commitment to the values of hard work, individual merit, and nondiscrimination.

Dea was understandably shocked when his own supervisors began directing him to bypass merit and to select for promotions the highest-ranking minority or female candidates, regardless of their relative qualifications. For Dea, who had never engaged in discrimination, that suggested course of action was offensive, even more so since the engineering positions for which he was selecting candidates were crucial to the health and sanitation interests of millions of people in suburban Washington. When Dea objected to illegally bypassing the highest-qualified candidates on the basis of race or gender, he was reprimanded. When he did so a second time, he was relieved of all supervisory duties. Those disciplinary actions, Dea's supervisor informed him, were intended to send a "shock wave" through the Commission and make sure no one else would deviate from the Commission's largely unwritten preference policies.

Dea's situation is unusual only because he had the courage to stand up for what he believes, even at tremendous personal cost. Around the nation, in both private and public firms, informal discrimination policies require for their success a "wink and a nod" from the people called on to implement them. Dea refused to wink and nod, for in so doing he would confer his moral imprimatur on a corrupt and fraudulent system.

51

The case of Stanley Dea illustrates many of the premises underlying the regime of racial preferences: that above a certain level of qualifications, people are fungible. That numbers determine racial outcomes. That failure to achieve numerical parity demonstrates discrimination. And that anyone who deviates from the prevailing orthodoxy must be dealt with severely. The quest for equal opportunity has been subverted in favor of racial entitlements, marking a dismal episode in the quest for civil rights.

It all started with noble intentions. The employment provisions of the Civil Rights Act were modest. Sen. Hubert Humphrey, the act's lead sponsor, emphasized that it "does not limit the employer's freedom to hire, fire, promote, or demote for any reasons—or for no reasons—so long as his action is not based on race."[2] In a dramatic moment, Humphrey declared that if anyone could find in the law "any language which provides that an employer will have to hire on the basis of percentage or quota . . ., I will start eating the pages one after another, because it is not in there."[3] Civil rights leaders were equally insistent that government stay out of the race-counting business. "The minute you put race on a civil service form," remarked NAACP lobbyist Clarence Mitchell at a White House conference in 1965, "you have opened the door to discrimination."[4]

But the terrain shifted quickly. Shelby Steele attributes the change to "a little-acknowledged yet extremely powerful effect of the civil-rights movement: the shame that marked America as it finally came to terms with its racial history." This shame dictated the evolution of civil rights policy:

> Social policymaking over the last 30 years was made by people and institutions lacking in moral authority to make principled decisions. Policy was made *defensively* to protect institutions from shame and the threat of legal action. Institutions that had discriminated now offered minorities the same group entitlements whites had long enjoyed.[5]

Those who advocated a shift from equal opportunity to equality of results knew they could never effectuate their agenda through the legislative process. But other means were now available: the civil rights groups now had at their disposal an extremely potent regulatory and law enforcement apparatus that they could manipulate toward markedly different objectives.

Of all the euphemisms the civil rights establishment has invoked over the years to describe its agenda in transforming equal employment opportunities into racial preferences, my favorite was coined by former EEOC chairperson Eleanor Holmes Norton: "conceptual innovations in equality mechanisms."[6] The conceptual innovations with the widest real-world ramifications in this area are two: "affirmative action" and "adverse impact." The first has been implemented primarily by executive orders and regulations, the second through court decisions. The goals and effects of both are identical: the redistribution of opportunities on the basis of race.

The concept of affirmative action inserted itself into public policy inconspicuously. President Lyndon Johnson made the case in a 1965 speech that something more than equal opportunity was necessary. "You do not take a person who has been hobbled by chains and liberate him, bring him to the starting line of a race and then say: 'You are free to compete with all the others,' " declared Johnson.[7]

That same year Johnson issued Executive Order 11246 to require government contractors to "take affirmative action to ensure that applicants are employed, and that employees are treated during employment, without regard to their race, color, religion, sex, or national origin." Given the order's clear nondiscrimination mandate, the term "affirmative action" could only mean race-neutral means to ensure equal opportunity and to create a level playing field for previously excluded people, such as recruitment and training programs, careful review of employment criteria and decisions, and so on.[8]

But in 1969, the U.S. Department of Labor adopted the mechanism of numerical "goals and timetables" to measure affirmative action, enforced through the Office of Federal Contract Compliance Programs. Soon thereafter, the federal government adopted regulations instructing employers that "[t]he rate of minority applicants recruited should approximate or equal the rate of minorities in the population of each location."[9] The racial quota regime had started.

Meanwhile, several federal agencies, including the Small Business Administration, began to interpret their mandate to provide assistance for "socially and economically disadvantaged" firms in a race-conscious manner. Through regulatory decrees, these agencies determined that certain specified groups were presumptively disadvantaged, whether or not they were so in fact. In practice these presumptions are irrebuttable. In this manner, race and gender set-asides for government contracts have come to permeate the federal government.[10] The federal government's power to create set-asides—and its authority, unlike state and local governments, to employ racial preferences to remedy "societal" discrimination—was sanctioned by the Supreme Court in *Fullilove v. Klutznick* in 1980,[11] and again in *Metro Broadcasting, Inc. v. FCC* in 1990.[12] Only with its 1995 decision in *Adarand Constructors, Inc. v. Pena*[13] did the Supreme Court finally begin applying the strictest constitutional scrutiny to federal programs, but by then the massive race preference structure had already been built.

At the same time, activists at the Equal Employment Opportunity Commission (EEOC), working in tandem with civil rights groups, began pushing legal theories that would dramatically expand the concept of discrimination embodied in the Civil Rights Act.[14] The concept was embraced by the Supreme Court in its 1971 decision, *Griggs v. Duke Power Co.*[15] Before 1971, plaintiffs in employment discrimination had two methods to prove their case. They could submit direct evidence of discriminatory intent (i.e., overt expressions of racism, the so-called "smoking gun"), or circumstantial evidence of "disparate treatment" (i.e., where two similarly situated persons are treated differently, giving rise to the inference that the explanation is race). In such cases of alleged intentional discrimination, an employer may rebut an inference of discrimination by articulating a nondiscriminatory reason for the decision, which the plaintiff may then attempt to discredit.

In *Griggs*, the Court sanctioned a third method of establishing a claim of discrimination, "adverse impact"—that is, where a particular employment criterion used by an employer yields different *outcomes* for different groups. Although applied by the Court in an innocuous way in *Griggs*, over the years the adverse impact concept would come to alter fundamentally the meaning of discrimination and to create a powerful engine of quotas.

*Griggs* involved a company that had ceased its prior discriminatory practices but thereupon adopted a requirement that job applicants possess either a high school diploma or a certain score on a standardized intelligence test. The Court found the salient facts as follows:

> (a) neither standard is shown to be significantly related to successful job performance, (b) both requirements operate to disqualify

Negroes at a substantially higher rate than white applicants, and (c) the jobs in question had been filled by white employees as part of a longstanding practice of giving preference to whites.[16]

Under these circumstances, even though the requirements were applied to blacks and whites equally, the Court had little difficulty finding that it unlawfully "operate[d] to 'freeze' the status quo of prior discriminatory employment practices."[17]

The decision in *Griggs* did not necessitate a radical departure from established legal principles. The use of statistics is an accepted means of demonstrating a covert intent to discriminate. But *Griggs* went a crucial further step: it suggested that the law was concerned with "the consequences of employment practices, not simply the motivation."[18] In other words, any employment standard that had an adverse impact on minorities could be held unlawful even if the employer did not use it for purposes of discrimination—indeed, even if the employer adopted such standards in order *not* to discriminate. In this way, adverse impact was used not only as a *method* of proving discrimination, but also as a new *definition* of discrimination. Indeed, adverse impact is sometimes described as proving "unconscious" discrimination, which is oxymoronic because the act of discrimination inherently involves a deliberate choice.

The EEOC and civil rights activists invoked adverse impact to attack a wide variety of employment standards, particularly tests. They were aided by a peculiar development in the law: in adverse impact cases (but, oddly, not in cases containing proof of discriminatory intent), the courts placed on the accused the burden of proving innocence; specifically, that the challenged standards were justified by "business necessity," a test nearly impossible to satisfy. Thus the anomaly that it became easier to prosecute—and more difficult to defend—cases based on statistics in which there was *no* evidence of discriminatory motivation than cases in which such evidence was presented. Put another way, cases in which employers treat similiarly situated people *differently* are easier to defend than cases in which employers treat people *alike*—which supposedly was the goal of the civil rights laws.

Adverse impact led also to a second anomaly: devices (such as tests) that remove subjectivity from employment decisionmaking—and that are explicitly authorized by the Civil Rights Act[19]—were successfully challenged and replaced by the very types of subjective decisionmaking that the Civil Rights Act was designed to diminish.[20] Though bizarre, those consequences are precisely what the civil rights groups wanted, for the groups are much more concerned with equal outcomes than with equal opportunity. That they convinced the courts to go along is quite remarkable.

Not surprisingly, the EEOC under then-Chairperson (now U.S. Representative) Eleanor Holmes Norton and the civil rights groups pursued adverse impact cases with gusto. Just as predictably, employers began insuring themselves against such lawsuits by getting their numbers right. Not just litigation but the specter of litigation—enormously costly and nearly impossible to defend against—ushered in the widespread use of racial preferences in private industry. Among other practices, private companies and government agencies began using "race norming"—adding points to the test scores of minorities to produce proportionate outcomes. In this way, employers could preserve some of the efficiency benefits of employment testing while avoiding exposure to legal challenges.

In their zeal to produce racial parity, the government litigators and their allies in the civil rights establishment lost sight of the original goal: eradicating discrimination. Individual complaints of discrimination, which by law must be filed first with the EEOC, languished or were summarily dismissed as Eleanor Holmes Norton devoted the EEOC's resources to high-impact statistical cases.

But eventually, the legal tide began to change. During the 1980s, one company refused to bow before EEOC pressure. Sears, Roebuck & Co. was accused by the EEOC of nationwide discrimination against women in hiring, promotion, and compensation in certain commission sales and management positions. Sears denied the charges. The case was based purely on numbers and resulted in a complex battle between statistical experts. The case cost both sides millions of dollars, at some points consuming one-third of the EEOC's entire litigation budget.[21] After six years of investigation by the EEOC, seven years of litigation, and 135 days of trial, the federal district court dismissed the lawsuit, finding it incredible that through all this the EEOC was unable to present a single individual who claimed she was a victim of discrimination.[22]

The legal terrain began to shift in the U.S. Supreme Court as well. In the 1986 decision in *Wygant v. Jackson Board of Education*, a majority of the Court for the first time applied the most stringent standard of constitutional scrutiny to government-erected racial preferences, striking down an explicit quota for teacher layoffs. Such extraordinary measures, Justice Lewis Powell declared, are permissible only if necessary to remedy the employer's own wrongdoing, predicated upon "particularized findings of past discrimination," without which "a court could uphold remedies that are ageless in their reach into the past, and timeless in their ability to affect the future."[23] Justice Powell explicitly rejected the "role model" justification offered by the school board, remarking that "[c]arried to its logical extreme, the idea that black students are better off with black teachers could lead to the very system the Court rejected in *Brown v. Board of Education.*"[24]

Three years later, applying the same "strict scrutiny" standard, the Court in *City of Richmond v. J.A. Croson Co.* struck down a 30 percent minority set-aside for public contracts on the grounds that the program was not narrowly tailored to remedy the city's past discrimination.[25] Though supporting the result, Justice Antonin Scalia criticized the majority for leaving intact the view that "despite the Fourteenth Amendment, state and local governments may in some circumstances discriminate on the basis of race."[26] As Scalia observed,

> The difficulty of overcoming the effects of past discrimination is as nothing compared with the difficulty of eradicating from our society the source of those effects, which is the tendency—fatal to a nation such as ours—to classify and judge men and women on the basis of their country of origin or the color of their skin. A solution to the first problem that aggravates the second is no solution at all.[27]

During this same period, the Court also reined in the adverse impact doctrine, bringing it more into line with other antidiscrimination legal theories. In its 1989 decision in *Wards Cove Packing Co. v. Atonio*,[28] the Court ruled that in adverse impact cases, (1) plaintiffs could not challenge the statistical "bottom line" of an employer's workforce, but must identify specific employment policies that cause racial imbalances by disqualifying minorities at a disproportionate rate; (2) plaintiffs, as in other types of cases, bear the burden of proof; and (3) employers may defend their employment practices by showing they serve legitimate business purposes in a significant way, rather than that they are essential or indispensable. A harsher rule, the Court observed, "would result in employers being potentially liable for the 'myriad of innocent causes that may lead to statistical imbalances in the composition of their work forces'."[29] The Court reasoned that "the only practicable option for many employers will be to adopt racial quotas, insuring that no portion of his work force deviates in racial composition from the other portions thereof; this is a result that Congress expressly rejected in drafting Title VII."[30]

*Wards Cove* sent the civil rights establishment into a frenzy, for it removed a crucial piston from the engine of quotas: it became considerably harder to wield the anti-discrimination law to coerce employers to discriminate to produce racial parity. Though the civil rights groups could do little to overturn the *Wygant* or *Croson* decisions because they were based on the Constitution, they could overturn *Wards Cove* by amending the Civil Rights Act of 1964.

A bitter struggle ensued, with supporters of the legislation calling *Wards Cove* a "rollback" of civil rights, and opponents (including President George Bush) denouncing it as a "quota bill." In the end the president capitulated (see Chapter 8) and signed the Civil Rights Act of 1991, which placed on defendants in adverse impact cases the burden of proving their business practices are "consistent with business necessity."[31] Fortunately, the law also expressly forbade race norming for the first time.

The combined effect of Supreme Court decisions and the Civil Rights Act of 1991 has created the following legal terrain: (1) government entities may engage in racial preferences only where necessary and narrowly tailored to remedy their own past discrimination; (2) private employers have somewhat wider latitude to engage in racial preferences to redress manifest statistical imbalances so long as they do not "unnecessarily trammel" job opportunities for nonminorities[32]; and (3) plaintiffs (including the government) may challenge employment practices that produce statistical imbalances. The substance is that despite the Fourteenth Amendment and the Civil Rights Act of 1964, both of which were supposedly colorblind, racial classifications continue to permeate the employment and business landscapes.

The reason is that even though the U.S. Supreme Court has narrowed the permissible range of discriminatory government policies, it has not interpreted either the Constitution or the Civil Rights Act in a colorblind manner. In his concurring opinion in *Croson*, Justice

Anthony Kennedy agreed with Justice Scalia that the "moral impera-
tive of racial neutrality is the driving force of the Equal Protection
Clause." But "on the assumption that it will vindicate the principle
of race neutrality," Justice Kennedy joined "the less absolute rule
contained in Justice [Sandra Day] O'Connor's opinion, a rule based
on the proposition that any racial preference must face the most
rigorous scrutiny by the courts."[33]

But the Court moved another step closer to construing the Constitution as colorblind with its decision in *Adarand Constructors* in 1995.
The Court took the unusual step of overturning key aspects of the
earlier *Fullilove* and *Metro Broadcasting* decisions, which had applied
a lower standard of review to federal than to state and local racial
preference programs. Writing for a 5–4 majority, Justice Sandra Day
O'Connor made clear that "all racial classifications . . . must be analyzed by a reviewing Court under strict scrutiny"[34]—a standard that
nearly always consigns challenged policies to demise. Justice Scalia
again urged the Court to go further:

> In my view, government can never have a "compelling interest" in
> discriminating on the basis of race in order to "make up" for past
> racial discrimination in the opposite direction. . . . Individuals who
> have been wronged by unlawful racial discrimination should be
> made whole; but under our Constitution there can be no such thing
> as either a creditor or a debtor race. . . . To pursue the concept of
> racial entitlement—even for the most admirable and benign of pur-
> poses—is to reinforce and preserve for future mischief the way of
> thinking that produced race slavery, race privilege and race hatred.
> In the eyes of the government, we are just one race here. It is Amer-
> ican.[35]

The civil rights groups reacted with predictable hysteria to the
Court's decision in *Adarand*. In typically temperate fashion, Jesse
Jackson denounced the ruling as "racist,"[36] adding that "while we
react to those wearing white sheets, it is those who wear black robes
who take away our protection."[37]

But the reaction is overblown. The decision did not remove a
single one of the 160 federal race preference programs, or otherwise
curb the government's racial discrimination policies. That task is
left to individual court challenges or federal legislation. And the
Court's majority, as in most recent civil rights decisions, rests on
the thread of a single vote.

More significant, although the Court has made known its disdain for racial preferences and its intention to strike down most if not all such programs, its failure to embrace the principle of a colorblind Constitution leaves the door open to policymakers bent on perpetuating a racial spoils system. And as history amply has demonstrated, anything less than an absolute principle of nondiscrimination will lead to exceptions that devour the rule. And so government acting as law enforcer, regulator, and purveyor of benefits and opportunities continues inexorably to expand the regime of racial preferences.

To what effect? Perhaps the costs of race-based affirmative action might be worth it if the policy had succeeded in dramatically raising up the most disadvantaged members of society, or in boosting productivity or prosperity, or in healing racial divisions. Sadly, affirmative action policies have failed on each of those important measures.

They certainly have not aided economic productivity. Defenders of affirmative action insist that its beneficiaries are not "unqualified." This suggests that above a certain minimal level of competence, people are fungible, therefore making it essentially costless to choose people on the basis of factors other than qualifications. But in fact racial preferences ignore relative qualifications, leapfrogging less-qualified people over better-qualified ones by whatever standard of merit would otherwise apply. And the purpose of the civil rights laws was precisely to remove racial considerations from the definition of merit.

Predictably, such deviations from the highest standards result in diminished efficiency and productivity. Quantifying the economic costs of racial preferences is difficult. But there is no denying such costs are substantial. Economist Farrell Bloch estimates that costs of affirmative action compliance and productivity losses among private firms that contract with the federal government alone total $40 billion annually.[38] Peter Brimelow and Leslie Spencer calculate the costs of race-based affirmative action at as much as 4 percent of the gross national product—about as much as we spend on the entire public school system.[39]

In preferences bestowed directly by the government, a large share of the cost consists of set-asides for companies that supposedly are minority-owned. In 1993, the federal government awarded $10.5 billion to minority-owned firms, half pursuant to Small Business Administration set-asides and most of the remainder under contracting goals of other agencies. This total was more than twice $5 billion spent on the federal school lunch program. Although set-asides are supposed to give disadvantaged firms a hand-up into the contracting business, the evidence suggests a more destructive tendency. The *Rocky Mountain News* tracked 100 companies that in 1985 received contracts under the city of Denver's affirmative action program that set aside 16 percent of contracts to provide a "temporary" boost for minority-owned firms. Ten years later, 42 had gone out of business, 34 were still dependent on the program, and only 24 are still in business and no longer part of the program.[40]

Nor has the massive governmental investment in preference programs apparently increased the overall number of jobs for minorities. The black-to-white unemployment ratio has actually widened since enactment of the Civil Rights Act: in 1964, about twice as many blacks were unemployed as whites; by 1990, the ratio was 2.76 unemployed blacks for every unemployed white worker.[41]

The economic status of blacks relative to whites increased substantially between 1965 and 1975, but the gap has persisted since that time, despite massive antidiscrimination and affirmative action efforts.[42] But the gains apparently are not attributable to outcome-based civil rights strategies. Since the federal law enforcement apparatus had not yet geared up during the period of significant black economic gains—the EEOC did not even have power to sue until 1972—the most likely explanations for the economic advances of blacks in the first 10 years following the Civil Rights Act, apart from educational advances, are the elimination of Jim Crow laws and a change in the behavior of employers, particularly in the South.[43] As Richard Epstein observes, the principal effect of the civil rights laws during this period was to "increas[e] the scope of market activities. The successes of the civil rights movement derived from the shrinkage, not the expansion, of total government power, both state and federal."[44] By contrast, after 1975, despite much more intensified litigation and enforcement—along with deployment of adverse impact cases and numerical remedies—blacks as a group made no further economic gains.[45]

A recent study by two proponents of affirmative action confirms the paltry gains attributable to government-coerced affirmative action. A survey of 138 firms by Alison M. Konrad and Frank Linnehan found that companies engaged in race-conscious employment policies had at least one woman at a higher rank and more minorities in management positions than those with race-neutral policies. But there was no difference in four other categories: the rank of the highest-ranking minority, the percentage of women in management, and the percentage of women and minorities in the company as a whole. The study found that companies using race-conscious policies were pressured into them by the government. Significantly, the researchers learned that most of the employees—including minorities and women—preferred systems that did not take race and gender into account. Despite the fact that such policies are unpopular and yield few tangible gains, the study's authors were undaunted: "We interpret these findings as indicating the importance of regulation for the imposition and inducement of unpopular organizational change," concluded Konrad and Linnehan. "External intervention appears to be needed to coerce organizations to adopt these structures."[46]

How can the meager employment gains be explained, given that governments at every level have been pursuing affirmative action and the OFCCP and EEOC have aggressively imposed quotas on private employers for more than 20 years? Despite the large costs, it turns out that those policies have had a mainly redistributionist impact: affirmative action primarily has shifted workers from some employers to others, rather than bringing new entrants into the workforce.[47]

Moreover, the civil rights laws had the perverse effect of making the irrational more rational: hiring minority employees exposed employers to the risk of discrimination claims for termination or other grievances. That induced some employers not to hire minority employees and others to move to the suburbs.[48] Those disincentives, along with social factors such as welfare dependency, inner-city isolation, inadequate education, and crime have for the past two decades neutralized any economic gains for blacks as a group wrought by race-based affirmative action. The crucial point about the economic record is this: affirmative action has mainly been about redistributing opportunities, and has failed utterly to increase the pool of qualified workers capable of competing effectively for economic opportunities. This is the fraud of affirmative action.

In economic parlance, we have pursued "demand side" affirmative action, which involves providing preferences to those who possess skills and resources, while ignoring "supply side" affirmative action, in which the pool of qualified individuals is expanded. The former, which merely involves redistribution, is easy but superficial in its real-world benefits. The latter, which involves removing barriers to educational opportunities and other facets of individual empowerment, is much more difficult but ultimately far more productive.

Race-based affirmative action also has imposed serious social costs. Most obvious is the racial polarization that results inevitably from racial discrimination. In their study of racial attitudes, Paul M. Sniderman and Thomas Piazza found that "the new race-conscious agenda has provoked broad outrage and resentment. Affirmative action is so intensely disliked that it has led some whites to dislike blacks—an ironic example of a policy meant to put the divide of race behind us in fact further widening it."[49] The policies not only foster resentment, but reinforce negative stereotypes. As Sniderman and Piazza discovered in their polling, "whites have come to think less of blacks, to be more likely to perceive them as irresponsible and lazy merely in consequence of the issue of affirmative action being brought up."[50]

The beneficiaries of racial preferences also suffer in more subtle yet debilitating ways. For hiring by race instead of merit undermines the commitment to excellence, for which there is no substitute. Racial preferences, by contrast, are a kind of narcotic, luring beneficiaries into an addictive dependency, sapping their spirit and pride. In the process we have lost sight of an essential truth: there is no shortcut to success.

This is far from what the original proponents of the civil rights laws had in mind. As Martin Luther King Jr. proclaimed in 1960,

> Doors are opening now that were not open in the past, and the great challenge facing minority groups is to be ready to enter these doors as they open. No greater tragedy could befall us at this hour but that of allowing new opportunities to emerge without the concomitant preparedness to meet them.
>
> We must make it clear to our young people that this is an age in which they will be forced to compete with people of all races and nationalities. We cannot aim merely to be good Negro teachers, good Negro doctors, or good Negro skilled laborers. We must set out to do a good job irrespective of race. We must seek to do our job so well that nobody could do it better.[51]

Compare these sentiments with the observations of Princeton professor Carol Swain on the effects of race-based affirmative action:

> As a successful black academic who has had to overcome the dis-
> advantages of an impoverished rural Virginia background, I have
> seen how affirmative action policies can have the paradoxical effect
> of undermining initiative and self-confidence. In a society with a
> history of egregious racism and sexism, it is all too easy for members
> of racial and ethnic minorities, particularly if they are women, to
> play the role of helpless victim. . . . But the role of helpless victim,
> while seductive, is pernicious in its effects. Victims view the world
> as menacing and hostile, and their defensiveness often undermines
> that wellspring of personal initiative and self-assurance required for
> sustained achievement.[52]

Shelby Steele puts the matter just as bluntly, asserting that through
the prevailing orthodoxy young blacks

> are taught that extra entitlements are their due and that the greatest
> power of all is the power that comes to them as victims. If they
> want to get anywhere in American life, they had better wear their
> victimization on their sleeve and tap into white guilt, making whites
> want to escape by offering money, status, racial preferences—some-
> thing, anything—in return. Is this the way for a race that has been
> oppressed to come into its own? Is this the way to achieve indepen-
> dence?[53]

Closely related is the stigma that attaches from preferences, not
only to their beneficiaries but also to everyone in the preferred
group.[54] As Carol Swain observes, "affirmative action policy tele-
graphs an equally harmful subliminal message to its beneficiaries.
It says in effect that you, as a woman or a minority, are less capable
than a white male and will need special preference in order to
compete successfully in a world dominated by white males."[55]
Indeed, the presumption has become pervasive that a minority individual or woman occupying a successful position could not have
achieved that status on merit alone. In the past year, I can hardly
recall a single debate over affirmative action in which blacks or
women who are critical of such policies are not accused of being
ungrateful beneficiaries. What a patronizing and demeaning
assumption! Yet it is a necessary corollary of group identification
and preferences.

But the most devastating cost of racial preferences is that they
treat the symptoms, not the causes, of racial disparities. The premises
underlying adverse impact were flawed from the outset—given the

wide range of individual talents and choices, we cannot expect members of all groups to be evenly distributed in all walks of life, even absent discrimination. Yet almost any time women or minorities are "underrepresented," whether in corporate boards or elite institutions of higher learning, the reflexive response is that something is wrong, and that "something" must be discrimination. The problem with this reflex is that when it is false—when the explanation is not discrimination—then to treat it as discrimination is to leave the real problem unsolved and unaddressed.

Indeed, if statistics ever told us much about discrimination, their relevance certainly is diminished today. Not only because discrimination is less common, though unquestionably it is, but also because factors other than discrimination increasingly explain statistical disparities. So long as we deny this fact, the disparities will persist no matter how much racial redistribution we do.

Take the example of Chicago. In the 1960s, if an employer hired few minority workers into entry-level jobs, the explanation probably was discrimination. Today, the explanation probably would not be discrimination, but rather the Chicago public schools. Half the students in the Chicago public schools drop out before graduating. Of the half who remain, 50 percent take college entrance exams. Despite this high attrition rate, the results are abysmal: 38 of Chicago's 64 high schools rank in the bottom 1 percent nationally on college entrance exams. Only one high school of 64 ranks at the 50th percentile or above.[56]

What this all means is that out of 400,000 mostly minority students in the Chicago public schools, almost none will graduate with the most basic skills necessary for college or productive livelihoods. Yet under the adverse impact paradigm, an employer whose entry-level workforce reflects this dismal reality will be held liable for discrimination and forced to adopt quotas. Faced with this dilemma, the employer will lure away qualified minority candidates from other companies, lower its hiring standards—or move out of Chicago.

This scenario repeats itself in every city every day. For so long as 20 percent of black students nationally do not graduate from high school, 88 percent of black high school graduates are not proficient in reading skills, 72 percent of black students drop out of college, and three-fourths of young black male high school dropouts have criminal records (see Chapter 1), racial preference programs cannot substantially improve the status quo. As William Julius Wilson demonstrated in *The Truly Disadvantaged*, "the factors associated with the growing woes of low-income blacks are exceedingly complex and go beyond the narrow issue of contemporary discrimination." As a consequence, race-based policies, while "beneficial to more advantaged blacks," says Wilson, "do little for those who are truly disadvantaged."[57]

Race-based affirmative action, by definition, can assist only those who have the skills or capital to come to the starting gate. Examples of affirmative action as a naked racial spoils system for the best-off members of minority groups are all too common and increasingly perverse.[58] *Forbes* magazine recently publicized the example of the Fanjul brothers, Cuban immigrants and strong financial backers of Bill Clinton who have made more than $500 million in the sugar cane business in southern Florida. As a spinoff company, they launched a low-capital finance company that, due to the brothers' Hispanic heritage, has been able to cash in on hundreds of thousands of dollars in minority set-asides.[59]

Many set-asides involve the Federal Communications Commission, which lavishly dishes out subsidies for wealthy minority-owned companies. The now-famous Viacom deal—the first racial preference ever repealed by Congress—involved a tax break given to companies only when they sold broadcast licenses to minority-owned firms. In this case, the firm buying the license was prepared to pay $2 billion[60]—hardly an amount that can be raised by a company that is in any sense disadvantaged. When the policy was discontinued, Sen. Carol Moseley-Braun (D-Ill.) proposed an exemption to protect a $12 million tax break that was being passed along from Rupert Murdoch to the purchasers of one of his television stations— the *Chicago Tribune* Company and wealthy music producer Quincy Jones (whose participation qualified the company for minority-owned status).[61]

Affirmative action—or a preference program for the well-connected? It is refreshing to hear voices now raised among defenders of the status quo against "abuses" and "excesses" (though such concerns ring hollow in some quarters, particularly among the Congressional Black Caucus, which tenaciously defended the Viacom tax breaks). But the true "abuses" of racial preferences are found not in how wealthy the beneficiaries are, but in the very act of racial discrimination itself. That is why "reviews" of affirmative action to ferret out abuses and excesses are ultimately pointless, for the entire preference regime is inherently corrupt.

Investing massive societal resources in racially divisive policies that help those group members with the greatest skills and resources—and who probably could make it without government intervention—makes little sense. A race-based scholarship, a job quota, a business set-aside, a multi-million-dollar tax break for wealthy entertainers—none of these has the remotest relevance to those in whose name affirmative action policies are invoked.

Some defenders of the status quo argue that affirmative action was never intended to aid the disadvantaged, but instead was intended to counter discrimination. And yet it is the statistical underrepresentation of minorities—in corporate boardrooms, colleges, professions—that is constantly invoked to demonstrate the continued need for preferences. "Access is still very limited, and the numbers are still very low," declares Columbia law professor Patricia Williams, a defender of preferences.[62]

But because the inability of the disadvantaged to compete for jobs or college admissions contributes heavily to this underrepresentation, what we have are policies justified by the existence of people who are outside the economic mainstream, yet who do not receive the benefits. As social scientist Glenn Loury remarks, "The suffering of the poorest blacks creates, if you will, a fund of political capital upon which all members of the group can draw when pressing racially based claims."[63]

We are swiftly arriving at a time, if we are not already there, when minority individuals who possess good academic credentials will have no difficulty securing job or educational opportunities. To the extent they find discriminatory barriers blocking their paths, the anti-discrimination laws are adequate to the task of removing them. Preferences for those who already possess skills and resources are unnecessary surplus baggage.

This does not mean it is wrong to give a helping hand to people who have had to overcome disadvantages; indeed, many members of minority groups have had to surmount obstacles that few of us can even imagine, and certainly it is legitimate to take such factors into account on an individual basis. But race is not a suitable proxy for disadvantage. The record of government in attempting to ensure equality of results through income redistribution is a disastrous one, a point that even some liberals now seem willing to concede.[64] In the universe of failed redistributionist policies, apportioning opportunities by race seems the crudest means of all.

The cost of preferences, to both victims and beneficiaries, vastly outweighs their illusory benefits. We need to end the fraud of affirmative action, and begin solving the real problems that prevent the truly disadvantaged from earning a share of the American Dream.

# 5. Education: Separate and Unequal

It always is gratifying to see a truly deserving person beat the odds. An important part of the American tradition is that talent and hard work so often prevail over status and privilege.

So it seemed for Cheryl Hopwood, a woman whose hard work appeared about to pay off when she applied in 1992 for admission to law school at the University of Texas. Until, that is, she encountered the most pernicious obstacle government can place in a person's path: a barrier that denied her dream on the basis of race.

Cheryl Hopwood is a certified public accountant who worked 20 to 30 hours per week while earning her undergraduate degree from California State University, where she was active in the Big Brothers and Big Sisters charity. She asked to attend law school on a limited basis for her first year so she could care for her child, who was born with cerebral palsy.

Hopwood had compiled excellent academic credentials. Her 3.8 undergraduate grade-point average and 39 Law School Aptitude Test score (which combined for a weighted "Texas Index" rating of 199) qualified her for presumptive admission. Only one black candidate for admission had a Texas Index rating as high as Hopwood's, and three Mexican-Americans had the same rating; all were admitted.

But Hopwood was denied admission. Thereafter, she and three other unsuccessful white candidates sued the university for discrimination. Evidence at trial revealed a sophisticated process for achieving minority admission goals—not by taking into account individual merit or disadvantage, but by lowering standards for minority applicants. Under the system, an applicant with a Texas Index score of 189 would be well within the presumptive denial range for whites—but within the presumptive admission range for minorities. Moreover, applications of minority candidates ranked in the discretionary range were reviewed by a minority admissions subcommittee, which used different procedures than are applied to nonminority candidates in the discretionary range.

The trial court acknowledged that minority students in Texas on average have lower credentials and higher high school and college dropout rates, which leads to a diminished pool of qualified minority candidates. Still, the court concluded that preferential admissions policies were necessary to fulfill the state's "compelling interest" in remedying past discrimination and "obtaining the educational benefits that flow from a racially and ethnically diverse student body."[1]

But the court concluded that the mechanism of separately evaluating minority and nonminority candidates—rather than according race a "plus" factor—was unlawful.[2] The court enjoined the use of separate admissions procedures, but ruled that Hopwood and her fellow plaintiffs (three white male students) had not demonstrated they would have been admitted absent the discriminatory policies. For her troubles, the court awarded Cheryl Hopwood nominal damages of one dollar.

Turning Cheryl Hopwood away from the University of Texas law school in favor of a less-qualified candidate who was not even born during the era of state-sanctioned discrimination seems a perverse remedy for past injustices. Though the court expressed discomfort with the use of race-based policies, ultimately its decision rested on a distinction without a difference: giving race a "plus" factor will yield exactly the same results as using separate lists. Everything else about the system the court endorsed is likewise the same: admissions officials judge candidates on the basis not of individual characteristics but of race, better-qualified candidates lose out to less-qualified ones, and the procedure foments racial division—but it does little to solve underlying social problems that contribute to racial disparities.

Perhaps nowhere has the transformation in civil rights policy from equal opportunity to the self-defeating goal of racial balance borne more devastating human consequences than in education. Indeed, as was illustrated by the case of Mark Anthony Nevels in Chapter 1, misguided civil rights remedies have played a central role in the denial of equal educational opportunities to children who need them most.

That this is so is particularly sobering from a historical perspective. Recognizing that education is a requisite for individual achievement, the civil rights movement from the earliest part of this century

70

made securing equal educational opportunities its top priority. An antecedent to *Brown v. Board of Education* was a 1908 case involving Berea College, a private institution that had been assessed a $1,000 fine for violating Kentucky's segregation laws. Southern white supremacists viewed private schools as organs of racial integration and were determined to use the coercive power of the state to squelch such free association. Berea College appealed the fine assessed against it for violating segregation laws, but the U.S. Supreme Court upheld the decision. As he had in *Plessy v. Ferguson*, Justice John Harlan dissented, declaring that "the statute is an arbitrary invasion of the rights of liberty and property guaranteed by the Fourteenth Amendment against hostile state action."[3] Harlan plaintively queried his countrymen,

> Have we become so inoculated with prejudice of race that an American government, professedly based on the principles of freedom, and charged with the protection of all citizens alike, can make distinctions between such citizens in the matter of their voluntary meeting for innocent purposes simply because of their respective races?[4]

Decisions like these gave impetus to the NAACP to pursue a systematic, case-by-case campaign to abolish state-sanctioned segregation in education, and eventually the Supreme Court began to strike down race-based educational barriers. In 1950, the Court invalidated a state rule requiring a black college student to sit separately from whites in classes, the library, and the cafeteria. Acknowledging that the "removal of the state restrictions will not necessarily abate individual and group predilections, prejudices and choices," the Court ruled that the state nonetheless may not deprive a person of "the *opportunity* to secure acceptance by his fellow students on his own merits."[5]

These rulings paved the way for a frontal assault on the doctrine of "separate but equal" in public education. In *Brown*, Thurgood Marshall argued for an absolute standard of colorblindness, declaring that

> so far as our argument on the constitutional debate is concerned . . ., the state is deprived of any power to make any racial classification in any governmental field. . . . It is the dissenting opinion of Justice Harlan, rather than the majority opinion in *Plessy v. Ferguson*, that is in keeping with the scope and meaning of the Fourteenth Amendment.[6]

Marshall made it absolutely clear he was not demanding racial balance, but merely the eradication of segregation: "If the lines are drawn on a natural basis, without regard to race or color, then I think that nobody would have any complaint." The NAACP Legal Defense Fund's Jack Greenberg was even more explicit, declaring that if "there were complete freedom of choice, or geographical zoning, or any other nonracial standard, and all Negroes still ended up in certain schools, there would seem to be no constitutional objection."[7]

The Supreme Court gave Marshall the outcome he wanted, but not the reasoning. Education, the Court declared, "where the state has undertaken to provide it, is a right which must be made available to all on equal terms."[8] But it refused to embrace a colorblind standard, instead applying essentially the same standard of reasonableness that was used 58 years earlier to sustain "separate but equal" in *Plessy*. Rather than deciding the case on the right of black schoolchildren to be treated as individuals and not segregated on the basis of their skin color, the Court relied upon the sociological effects of segregation to strike down the law. "To separate [black children] from others of a similar age and qualifications solely because of their race," the unanimous Court propounded, "generates a feeling of inferiority as to their status in the community that may affect their hearts and minds in a way unlikely ever to be undone."[9] The Court's grounding of its decision in sociology and its failure to forthrightly overturn *Plessy* and repudiate government's power to discriminate are a source of the confusion over civil rights that has followed.[10]

Nowhere were the ramifications of this failure more pronounced and devastating than in the area of education. Nathan Glazer provides an all-too-accurate summary:

> Constitutional law often moves along strange and circuitous paths, but perhaps the strangest yet has been the one whereby, beginning with an effort to expand freedom—no black child shall be excluded from any public school because of his race—the law has ended up with as drastic a restriction of freedom as we have seen in this country in recent years: No child, of any race or group, may "escape" or "flee" the school to which that child has been assigned on the basis of his or her race.[11]

How did a movement that started out with such promise end up contradicting its very objectives? As in the other main areas of civil

rights law enforcement, mistakes were born of impatience
to the adoption of goals and use of tools that undermined the origin...
mission. As elsewhere, the goal shifted from desegregation and equal
opportunity to racial balance. The mechanism chosen to effectuate
this goal was forced busing, in whose wake lie the carnage of inner-
city public school systems and the hopes and dreams of thousands
of American schoolchildren.[12]

Perhaps in no other area was opposition to civil rights more intense
than in the desegregation of public schools. Images of southern
governors such as Orval Faubus and George Wallace blocking the
schoolhouse doors—of James Meredith crossing the threshold of the
University of Mississippi with an armed escort—provided national
symbols not only of massive resistance but also of the stern measures
that plainly would be necessary to ensure equal opportunity. But
despite the Supreme Court's admonition in 1955 that school systems
must desegregate with "all deliberate speed,"[13] a decade after *Brown*,
only 2.3 percent of black public school students in the South were
attending desegregated schools,[14] and not a single black child was
attending a public school with white children in South Carolina,
Alabama, or Mississippi.[15]

But instead of providing relief to victims of discrimination—
indeed, despite her "victory," Linda Brown graduated from an all-
black school in Topeka[16]—or undoing segregated pupil assignments
and forbidding racial discrimination, the courts in the mid-1960s
began ordering racial balance in accordance with guidelines issued
by the U.S. Department of Health, Education and Welfare.[17] From
that time on, the federal courts became enmeshed in school governance in hundreds of cities around the country, displacing local
school authorities over such matters as student assignments, trans-
portation, finance, educational policies, and testing[18]—and even such
matters as pay raises for janitors and cafeteria workers.[19]

But the overarching touchstone was racial balance. As the columnist William Raspberry has observed, the civil rights groups "became
almost monomaniacally concerned with the maximum feasible mix-
ing of races, with educational concerns a distant second."[20] In its
1971 ruling in *Swann v. Charlotte-Mecklenburg Board of Education*, the
Supreme Court approved the ordering of racial ratios, race-based
teacher reassignments, altered attendance zones, and forced busing,
affirming the trial court's finding that "in order to live in a pluralistic

73

society each school should have a prescribed ratio of Negro to white students reflecting the proportion for the district as a whole."[21] Two years later it approved such remedies even in school districts where students never had been assigned on the basis of race.[22]

The Supreme Court slowly but fairly steadily has begun scaling back the federal judiciary's power in this area, refusing under some circumstances to allow forced busing into the suburbs[23] or constant court-ordered changes in student assignment ratios.[24] The Court repeatedly in recent years has instructed lower courts that they may not remain in the desegregation business forever, and that school districts cannot be held responsible for racial demographics they did not cause.[25] And yet, busing for desegregation is still imposed in hundreds of cities, often operating under court orders more than two decades old.[26] Indeed, the *Brown* case itself still awaits final resolution after more than *40 years* of litigation![27]

Even if the courts return control to local school officials, the damage is done. Forced busing triggered a devastating chain reaction from which many school districts have never recovered. In city after city, busing led to massive "white flight" (or, more accurately, middle-class flight") away from public schools to private schools or the suburbs[28]—not always for racial reasons, but to keep children close to home and out of bad schools. As a consequence, school districts (particularly in the inner cities) became predominantly minority, with black and Hispanic students bearing the brunt of busing in an increasingly futile search for white students. Transporting children away from their neighborhood schools led to diminished parental involvement in their children's education. And with the exodus of middle-class parents, both the tax base and public support for the public schools eroded. What perverse consequences flow from unbridled social engineering, with little children playing the role of mice in the social laboratory: the schools are often nearly as segregated as ever, but while middle-class children have escaped, the children for whom this "remedy" was imposed are left behind in decaying, defective schools.[29]

For all this there has been no attendant gain in black student achievement. Whatever gains black students have made are attributable to socioeconomic advances among black families and to "voluntary" desegregation measures such as magnet schools, whereas desegregation through busing has produced negligible if any academic gains.[30] Undeterred, civil rights activists have pressed for even greater judicial intervention, such as busing into the suburbs and increased educational spending.

But just as busing has little to commend it as an educational policy, neither does increased spending.[31] A review of 187 studies found that "there is no systematic relationship between school expenditures and school performance."[32] The Kansas City school desegregation litigation, which has been going on since 1977, provides a prime example. Federal judge Russell Clark ordered a gold-plated remedy that so far has cost taxpayers $1 billion and raised per-pupil costs to 2.5 times the statewide average. The court-ordered program has produced such amenities as swimming pools, greenhouses, an art gallery and screening room, an animation lab and a planetarium—but no improvement in student achievement.[33]

Fearing that Judge Clark's power to micromanage the schools might be terminated, the plaintiffs' lawyers argued in the Supreme Court that test scores should be the measure of compliance with the desegregation decree—a measure that would likely perpetuate judicial control forever. In 1995, the Supreme Court, by a vote of five to four, disagreed. Constant judicial intervention in the school district's governance beyond the narrow task of dismantling state-enforced segregation, the Court ruled, strays beyond the permissible bounds of judicial power.[34] "The District Court must bear in mind," wrote Chief Justice William Rehnquist, "that its end purpose is not only "to remedy the violation' to the extent practicable, but also "to restore state and local authorities to the control of a school system that is operating in compliance with the Constitution.' "[35] Justice Clarence Thomas's concurring opinion went to the heart of the matter:

> The point of the Equal Protection Clause is not to enforce strict race-mixing, but to ensure that blacks and whites are treated equally by the State without regard to their skin color. The lower courts should not be swayed by the easy answers of social science, nor should they accept the findings, and the assumptions, of sociology and psychology at the price of constitutional principle.[36]

It appears some lower courts are getting the message. In Denver, federal judge Richard Matsch in 1995 finally allowed the school system to end busing after 21 years of judicial control and repeated pleas by a school board that in recent years has had black and Hispanic presidents. "The Denver now before this court is very different from what it was when this lawsuit began," observed Judge Matsch. Thanks to busing, the schools have deteriorated and the number of white students has declined from over 63,000 in 1968 to 18,000 today. Donna Good, education assistant to Mayor Wellington Webb, says, "Black neighborhoods were also shattered by busing." Now, at least, the city can return to neighborhood schools and begin picking up the pieces.[37]

None of the recent court defeats has chastened the purveyors of race balancing. "Civil rights groups are back in court, not only to oppose unitary status but to demand even broader remedies than those granted during the 1970s," observes David Armor. "They have requested metropolitan remedies between cities and suburbs, and they have petitioned for racial parity in classrooms, discipline rates, and even academic achievement."[38]

But it is clear that among mainstream Americans, (both white and black), patience for such nonsense has stretched thin. When the Minneapolis NAACP announced recently a desegregation lawsuit seeking integration across school district lines, a poll found that residents favored neighborhood schools over racial balance by a margin of 75 to 16 percent.[39]

Indeed, the use of racial classifications continues unabated in the service of social engineers. In affluent Montgomery County, Maryland, Mary Yee and Warren Maruyama tried to take advantage of the school district's public school "choice" program by transferring their daughters from Takoma Park Elementary School to a French language immersion school. Yee and her husband are multilingual and travel frequently to French-speaking countries; Muruyama and his wife studied French and wanted their daughter to learn a second language. The school seemed perfect for their little girls.

But their applications were denied—not because of qualifications or the luck of draw, but because the girls are of Asian ethnicity. Even though they are under no compulsion to do so, the Montgomery public schools maintain ethnic balance policies for each of the schools. In this case, the transfer was denied because only 11 of 519 students at Takoma Park are classified as Asian, and the girls' departure would increase the "ethnic isolation" of the remaining Asian students. "It's clear what you have here is a thinly disguised system of racial quotas."

Undaunted by the transfer denial, Yee tried a new tack: because her husband is white, she changed her daughter's official racial classification to white and applied again. But again school officials thwarted the effort, this time citing a policy that discourages transfers out of schools undergoing significant enrollment changes. So the girls were denied a place in the school their parents preferred solely on account of their race. "It's painful to hear you cannot get into one of the programs Montgomery County is famous for just because you're Asian," laments Maruyama.[40]

Despite the massive societal resources invested in desegregation and other schemes, for minority children the educational landscape is bleak. As Charles Murray reported in *Losing Ground*, by 1980 "the gap in educational achievement between black and white students was so great that it threatened to defeat any other attempts to narrow the economic differences separating blacks and whites."[41] The news is little better 15 years later (see Chapters 1 and 4).

Not surprisingly, the deficiencies at the elementary and secondary levels of education produce a trickle-up effect in higher education, manifesting themselves in poor credentials and low admissions numbers. The gaps between black and white applicants on college and graduate school admission tests are huge, with few blacks or Hispanics scoring in the top tiers.[42] At the University of Virginia, for instance, black students who are admitted score an average 240 points lower on the SAT than white students.[43] The stark reality is that if minority students, particularly from low-income families, continue to experience high dropout rates and low levels of academic achievement, we will continue to see widespread and massive "underrepresentation" of minorities in institutions of higher learning, particularly elite institutions.

Yet the response of government and educational institutions is not to solve the underlying problems but to sweep them under the carpet of racial preferences. The separate admissions track used by the University of Texas law school is hardly an innovation. In the 1970s, the approach of institutions of higher learning such as the medical school at the University of California at Davis was to substantially lower standards and to set aside a specific number of seats for minority applicants. These overt quotas were struck down by the 1978 *Bakke* decision, but, as would become a recurrent pattern, the Supreme Court limited but did not absolutely prohibit racial preferences.[44] As a result, today's preferences are often more subtle, even as they permeate the landscape of higher learning.

Some of the preferences are remarkably brazen, such as financial aid programs that are restricted to groups on the basis of race—in essence, 100 percent quotas. In 1989 Daniel Podberesky, a Hispanic student, was admitted to the University of Maryland. His academic credentials were excellent: he had a 4.0 high school grade-point average, scored 1340 out of a possible 1600 on the Scholastic Aptitude Test, and participated actively in extracurricular activities. He seemed a natural for scholarship assistance. The one program most geared to his credentials was the merit-based Banneker scholarship program, for which he was qualified in every way but one: the color of his skin.[45]

The University of Maryland has not discriminated since 1954. It provides a hospitable environment for minorities: 12 percent of its students are black, far above the 8 percent nationwide average; black students run their own lecture series and two newspapers; the campus is constructing a $3.7 million black cultural center. Yet claiming the need to remedy past discrimination and foster diversity, the college sets aside $1.2 million—15 percent of its state-supported unrestricted aid—solely for black students.[46] Striking down the program, the U.S. Court of Appeals for the Fourth Circuit declared, "Of all the criteria by which men and women can be judged, the most pernicious is that of race. The injustice of judging human beings by the color of their skin is so apparent that racial classifications cannot be rationalized by the casual invocation of benign remedial aims."[47]

Defenders of the status quo hysterically predict that if preferential admissions and scholarship programs are eliminated, minorities will disappear from colleges and universities. Indeed, the statistics are grim, particularly among elite institutions. A prime example is the University of California at Berkeley, which presently admits half its entering classes on the basis of grades and SAT scores, and the other half on the basis of "social diversity" factors. Its admissions officials estimate that elimination of racial preferences and reliance solely on academic credentials would reduce the proportion of black freshmen from 6.4 percent to between 0.5 and 1.9 percent, and the proportion of Hispanic freshmen from 15.3 percent to between 3.0 and 6.3 percent. The proportion of Asian-American freshmen at Berkeley would increase from 41.7 percent to as much as 54.7 percent, and the percentage of whites from 29.8 percent to as much as 37.3 percent.[48]

Still, the hysteria among advocates of racial preferences is overstated: there likely will be a redistribution of minority students from schools where students must rely on preferential policies to schools commensurate with their credentials. In other words, students currently admitted to Harvard might instead go to Boston University; those attending law school at Berkeley might find themselves at my alma mater, the University of California at Davis. Overall, though the change will be pronounced at the most elite universities, the numbers of minority students attending college probably will not decline significantly if at all as a result of curbing racial preferences.

In any event, preference policies may do their beneficiaries more harm than good. Race-based diminution of admissions standards inevitably causes a mismatch between students' abilities and the demands of the schools—a student scoring 240 points lower on the SAT, as is the case at the University of Virginia, is unlikely to be competitive. At Berkeley, for instance, a study found that half of black freshmen failed calculus courses, compared with 5 percent of Asian freshmen.[49] This mismatch may well contribute to a minority college dropout rate estimated nationally at an appalling 72 percent.[50] At Berkeley, the graduation rate for blacks is 37.5 percent, compared with 71.5 percent for whites.[51] If elimination of racial preferences leads to a closer match between skills and schools and reduces the dropout rate, the result might actually be a net *increase* in the number of minority students graduating from college.

For all sorts of reasons, race-based admissions and scholarship policies are a particularly clumsy form of social engineering. The essential problem is that race is not a proxy for anything—victimization, disadvantage, or diversity—that might be a justification for sound education-related policies. Race is both overinclusive and underinclusive—some people benefit who do not deserve to do so, while others who are more worthy do not benefit.

Those who defend such preferences retort that colleges have always had preferences, such as for athletes and children of alumni. As the son of a welder—and a person whose athletic prowess has yet to fully blossom—I am no great fan of such preferences.[52] But to sanction racial preferences by equating them with other types of preferences trivializes racial discrimination, which stands alone as the least-rational basis on which to apportion opportunities or render judgments.

Sadly, programs ostensibly designed to overcome racism and to promote "diversity" have too often had precisely the opposite effect. Colleges today frequently are racially polarized, with hostility flowing from both sides of the racial divide.[53] Political correctness, mandatory "sensitivity" training, self-segregated dormitories and academic programs, and preference policies all heighten race-consciousness and contribute to an intolerant environment. This in turn leads to demands for further race-based remedies that lead to greater polarization.[54]

In education as in so many other areas of public concern, the reflexive instinct is to explain every statistical disparity in terms of racism. But does anyone seriously believe that high-achieving black and Hispanic young men and women will be turned away from higher education today on the grounds of race or ethnicity by the very institutions that so eagerly engage in such preferences?

The real tragedy about racial preferences in education is that they do absolutely nothing to solve the real problems that cause minority underrepresentation in higher learning, which truly can be solved in only one way: by expanding the pool of highly qualified minority applicants. As with all such social engineering, racial preferences are redistributionist. They do not increase the storehouse of human capital, but merely spread around outcomes in a manner sure to be arbitrary, divisive, and fraudulent.

Surely, college officials are not going to abandon their propensities in this regard anytime soon, no matter how unequivocal the proscription. As Berkeley's chancellor Chang-Lin Tien glibly assures, even when racial preferences are forbidden, "We can come up with some tricks."[55]

If such officials are adamant about engaging in social leveling, at least let them do so in less noxious ways than racial discrimination. Colleges might gainfully look for students whose individual backgrounds suggest the ability to overcome adversity. A student who manages to graduate with a 3.0 grade-point average from a public high school in Compton, California, probably has as much raw talent as a student who graduated with a 3.5 from Beverly Hills. Moreover, such helping-hand assistance rendered on the basis of demonstrable merit or disadvantage comports with Americans' sense of fairness— just as racial preferences profoundly offend it.

But ultimately, the problems sought to be addressed by race-conscious educational policies—whether unequal educational opportunities at the elementary and secondary level, or underrepresentation in colleges and universities—can be addressed only through radical, systemic changes in our educational system. Racial preferences, for all the sound and fury, are not radical; they are reactionary and superficial. Yet ironically, many of the so-called civil rights leaders oppose the very reforms that would most greatly aid their purported beneficiaries.[56] I will discuss one essential reform, parental choice, in Chapter 10. But in closing this chapter, I hope one point is by now entirely clear, for our history cannot be more emphatic on this point: in the realm of education, so absolutely precious and vital to our society and to every child within it, racial classifications are a problem, not a solution.

# 6. Political Apartheid

Rarely does the United States Supreme Court write in vividly depictive terms, but the drawing of the congressional district lines before the Court in the 1993 *Shaw v. Reno* inspired it to wax both lyrical and comical.

Following the 1990 census, North Carolina's congressional district lines were redrawn to create two majority-black districts. The Court described the first, District 1, as

> somewhat hook-shaped. Centered in the northeast portion of the State, it moves southward until it tapers to a narrow band; then, with finger-like extensions, it reaches far into the southern-most part of the State near the South Carolina border. District 1 has been compared to a "Rohrscach inkblot test," . . . and a "bug splattered on a windshield."[1]

The other majority-black district, District 12, was

> even more unusually shaped. It is approximately 160 miles long and, for much of its length, no wider than the I-85 corridor. It winds in snake-like fashion through tobacco country, financial centers, and manufacturing centers "until it gobbles up enough enclaves of black neighborhoods." . . . One state legislator has remarked that "[i]f you drove down the interstate with both car doors open, you'd kill most of the people in the district."[2]

The bizarre districts at issue in *Shaw v. Reno* now dot the American political landscape, so much that they threaten to create what Justice Sandra Day O'Connor called a system of "political apartheid."[3] The districts are the product of a cynical collusion between the civil rights establishment, which wanted to increase minority political power, and the Republican National Committee, which wanted to segregate black voters to create more districts that would vote Republican.[4] In the 1992 and 1994 congressional elections, the strategy paid off for both with the election of more blacks and Republicans to Congress.

83

Demands by civil rights groups for racial gerrymandering rest upon several premises. Black voters, the proponents say, should be entitled to elect representatives of their choice. The number of black elected officials has increased dramatically in recent years, and that growth is attributable in large measure to the creation of "safe" districts. Minority political influence at both the federal and state levels has expanded commensurately. Moreover, gerrymandering is far from a new phenomenon in American politics[5]; it has been used throughout our history to protect incumbents, to advance the interests of political parties, and indeed to discriminate against blacks. If districts drawn to remedy past discrimination were invalidated, proponents warn, the number of elected minority officials would decline, erasing much of the progress of the past two decades.

Many of those premises are true or at least partly true. Yet none of the perceived benefits of racial gerrymandering outweighs the incalculable costs of dividing a society on the basis of race.

That is the direction in which we were headed, at least until the slender 5–4 majority in *Shaw v. Reno* ruled that deliberately gerrymandered election districts may violate the Constitution. But the Court refused to confront the fact that the problem is largely one of its own making, through 25 years of Voting Rights Act decisions that strongly encouraged racially proportionate political representation. As is the case with so many recent Supreme Court decisions, *Shaw* addressed the perverse consequences of its own jurisprudence while leaving intact the underlying precedents.

The Court took the corrective process a step further in 1995 with its decision in *Miller v. Johnson*. Following the 1990 census, the Georgia legislature, in a state whose population is 27 percent black, redrew district lines to increase from one (out of 10) to two (out of 11) majority-black congressional districts, creating a third that was 35 percent black. But the Justice Department was not satisfied, and joined forces with local advocacy groups to push for a so-called "max-black" plan to create a third majority-black district. The result was a district stretching 260 miles through rural farmlands to connect black enclaves in Savannah and suburban Atlanta—a district whose "social, political, and economic makeup," the Court observed, "tells a tale of disparity, not community."[6]

The Court by a 5–4 vote struck down the district lines as an unconstitutional racial gerrymander. Writing for the majority, Justice

Anthony Kennedy stressed that the goal of cleansing society and the political system of discrimination "is neither assured nor well served . . . by carving electorates into racial blocs."[7] The Georgia case illustrated well the polarizing impact of racial gerrymandering. Before the redistricting, Georgia's congressional delegation spanned the color and ideological spectrums. After the 1994 elections, it had three black Democrats and eight white Republicans.

As in the areas of employment and education, the regime of racial classifications that has developed in the voting rights area was not contemplated by the framers of the civil rights laws. The effort to ensure equal voting rights dates back to 1870 with ratification of the Fifteenth Amendment, which guaranteed that the "right of citizens of the United States" would not be "denied or abridged . . . by any State on account of race, color, or previous condition of servitude." But those who controlled the levers of power in a number of states devised unscrupulous schemes to indirectly thwart black voter participation, such as literacy tests, poll taxes, good character requirements, and racial gerrymandering.

To give meaning to the Fifteenth Amendment, Congress in 1965 passed the Voting Rights Act.[8] The act's preeminent historian, Abigail Thernstrom, observes that the "Voting Rights Act of 1965 had a simple aim: providing ballots for southern blacks."[9] Though its aim was modest, its sweep was not. The act covered jurisdictions, mostly in the South, that were considered suspect in discouraging access to the ballot. The substance of the act was section 2, which prohibited any discriminatory "voting qualification or prerequisite to voting, or standard, practice, or procedure."

But the act went further, creating a direct federal role in the governance of local political decisionmaking. Section 5 provided that any change to voting qualifications, prerequisites, standards, practices, or procedures would require "preclearance" by the Justice Department or the federal district court for the District of Columbia. In this way the act added to the Justice Department's law enforcement role a quasi-judicial function, making it both prosecutor and judge with respect to Voting Rights Act matters. As Thernstrom explains,

> The extraordinary power that the legislation conferred upon both the courts and the Department of Justice, permitting an unprecedented intrusion of federal authority into local electoral affairs, was meant

THE AFFIRMATIVE ACTION FRAUD

> to deal with an extraordinary problem: continued black disenfranchisement ninety-five years after the passage of the Fifteenth Amendment.[10]

As a consequence, these extraordinary powers were intended to be temporary and narrow.[11]

The act had an immediate impact in achieving its goal of securing access to the ballot: within two years, the proportion of blacks in Mississippi who were registered to vote increased from 6.7 percent to 59.8 percent, with large gains as well in other southern states.[12] But as Thernstrom observes, "As the emergency subsided, the emergency powers expanded,"[13] through court decisions, congressional amendment, and Justice Department interpretations.

The crucial step toward moving the Voting Rights Act beyond—and sometimes in contradiction to—its core objectives came quickly, with the Supreme Court's 1969 decision in *Allen v. State Board of Elections*. The questions presented to the Court involved whether such matters as moving from district to at-large elections for local supervisors constituted a change in voting "practices" or "procedures" requiring federal preclearance. In its first of successive decisions expanding the scope of section 2, the Court answered in the affirmative.

But the Court went much further than the narrow question presented, essentially rewriting the statute to far exceed its aim of securing access to the ballot. Writing for the majority, Chief Justice Earl Warren wrote that "the right to vote can be affected by a dilution of voting power as well as by an absolute prohibition on casting a ballot. . . . This type of change could therefore nullify [black voters'] ability to elect the candidate of their choice just as would prohibiting some of them from voting."[14]

In this manner, the Court made radical changes to the act. First, it introduced the concept of vote "dilution"—that somehow voting rights meant something more than being able to cast a vote, but rather a vote that is not "diluted." Second, it suggested that *groups* have a protected interest in electing "candidates of their choice"; in other words, a right to some sort of outcome.

But it was Justice John Harlan who noted in dissent the crucial dividing line the Court traversed in its decision, between whether to ensure equal opportunity or equality in results. "Under one system," he remarked, "Negroes have some influence in the election of all officers; under the other, minority groups have more influence in the selection of fewer officers."[15] In *Allen*, the Court committed itself firmly to the latter course, beginning the process, as Thernstrom observes, "by which the Voting Rights Act was reshaped into an instrument for affirmative action in the electoral sphere."[16]

Subsequent decisions and congressional amendments extended the reach of the Voting Rights Act to cover jurisdictions in Arizona, Alaska, New York City, and elsewhere; to include Mexican-Americans among the protected groups; and to extend its scope to redistricting and changes in political boundaries.[17] But the most sweeping change came in 1982, when Congress amended section 2 of the act to prohibit not only procedures that were intended to discriminate but also those that produced disproportionate "results."[18] Subsequent Supreme Court decisions held that changes that caused a "retrogression" in minority voting strength were illegal. All this led to a heavy focus on statistics in voting rights cases, featuring complex analyses of potential minority representation, intensity of racial bloc voting, and so forth.[19]

The 1982 amendments unleashed the Justice Department to exercise awesome new powers. Its preclearance authority, intended to protect against subterfuge, now extended to the utterly trivial, including changes in voter registration and hours of operation of registration sites. The result was that preclearance requests from covered jurisdictions that initially numbered in the hundreds grew by the mid-1980s to more than 10,000 annually.[20]

Far more pernicious, however, was the growing tendency of the Justice Department—particularly during the Bush Administration following the 1990 census—to use the preclearance power to coerce jurisdictions to "voluntarily" engage in racial gerrymandering. The Bush administration's assistant attorney general for civil rights, John Dunne, insisted that blacks were entitled to a "fair share" of political power.[21] Justice Department lawyers, working in close concert with civil rights advocacy groups, actually lobbied for specific redistricting plans to "maximize" black representation—in effect adding legislative functions to the executive and quasi-judicial powers the Justice Department already possessed.[22] The threat of denying preclearance of congressional redistricting and of tying up local jurisdictions in costly litigation proved an almost sure inducement to capitulation. The result was a massive effort, throughout the South and in other jurisdictions subject to the Voting Rights Act, to pack black and Hispanic voters into districts in such a way as to maximize the number of representatives from those groups.

Thus the result, parallel to other areas of civil rights law and policy, that a law designed to create equal opportunity and to remove barriers to an integrated society in fact has produced a pervasive system of racial classifications. And yet as law professor Andrew Kull remarks, "Among the . . . race-conscious means of achieving 'equality of results' . . ., the most radical innovation in terms of traditional American principles has inspired the least public controversy."[23] Racial gerrymandering does not evoke the same outrage as preferences in employment and education.

The explanation is simple: even though racial gerrymandering, like other racial classifications, is redistributionist, unlike other race-based policies, one person's gain does not necessarily lead to another person's loss. No one loses the right to vote, or his or her proportionate likelihood of electing a preferred candidate. Indeed, if the proponents have it right that voters prefer to vote for candidates of the same race, gerrymandered districts actually *increase* the likelihood of electoral satisfaction among many whites and blacks. This pragmatic argument translates into a legal one: no one has "standing" to challenge race-drawn districts, the proponents assert, since no one is injured.

So why is racial gerrymandering such a bad idea? Dissenting from a 1962 decision upholding Louisiana's requirement that candidates list their race on ballot papers, Judge John Minor Wisdom, who later would be considered the father of forced busing for his school desegregation decisions, declared, "If there is one area above all others where the Constitution is colorblind, it is the area of state action with respect to the ballot and the voting booth."[24] The reason is plain: American politics is the great melting pot. A minority cannot long be oppressed if the majority must court their votes. By contrast, if voters are segregated by race,[25] there is no need to take into account the minority's interests; they will achieve proportionate representation, but the number of representatives who are accountable to them in some way is diminished. Racial gerrymandering is a sure recipe for permanent balkanization of the American political landscape.

Racial gerrymandering is based on the premise that race defines interest. It is true that voters often vote for members of their own race, but it is increasingly less true. Racial considerations overlook the importance of economic status and ideology in ballot preferences. Middle-class black and white voters who reside in the same prosperous suburb surely have more in common than rural voters 260 miles away at the other end of the state, whether white or black; yet racial gerrymandering seeks to unite black voters, however different their individual interests. Moreover, just as whites span the ideological spectrum, so too are blacks represented fairly evenly among liberals, moderates, and conservatives.[26] Dividing voters by race will prevent voters who share characteristics other than race from coming together and will render ours a permanently divided nation.

By contrast, race-neutral line-drawing—districts drawn on the basis of natural political, geographic, or economic lines—tends to unite voters of truly similar interests, regardless of race. Moreover, far from the hysterical claims made by the civil rights establishment, minority representatives will not disappear in the absence of gerrymandering. Many districts drawn on race-neutral lines will be majority-minority; in many others, minorities will represent an influential constituency. In this way, while race-neutral districting will remove the current floor from minority officeholding, it will also lift the ceiling that is created by segregated line-drawing. Race-neutral districting also will increase the number of white officeholders who are accountable to minority voters—and minority officeholders who are accountable to white voters. In other words, politicians will be forced to transcend race if they hope to win elections.

The stakes in the field of electoral line-drawing are enormous, and the risks are amplified by the fact that the primary decision-makers often have a direct stake in the outcome. Skillfully manipulated, racial gerrymandering is a powerful engine for the redistribution of political power. Hardly anyone in the political realm, whether the Republican National Committee or the Congressional Black Caucus, seems immune from the temptation to manipulate electoral lines on the basis of race if it will increase their power base.

But the direction of voting rights policy bodes profound social and ideological ramifications as well, which is what precipitated the strong opposition to President Clinton's nomination of Professor Lani M. Guinier as assistant attorney general for civil rights. Guinier's nomination for the first time brought the real-world implications of voting rights policy into the center of American political debate.

89

Lani Guinier and I have some important things in common. Both of us aspired to careers as civil rights lawyers, and have toiled productively in the vineyards of public interest litigation. We both have spent most of our legal careers representing powerless minority individuals, and derive enormous personal fulfillment and inspiration from helping set matters right. Perhaps most significantly, we care greatly about ideas, and understand that in today's society lawyers armed with the right ideas have the power to change the world.

So it was not without a degree of admiration that I first explored the corner of the ideological world Lani Guinier inhabits—but in that process I grew gravely concerned about how those ideas would translate into reality, through the powerful apparatus of the Justice Department's Civil Rights Division.

We are not without agreements. There are enough kernels of insights in Guinier's writings to make the typical reader nod in agreement. Guinier, for instance, acknowledges that racial gerrymandering is divisive and limits electoral opportunities for minorities. And her principal premise—that minorities (racial or otherwise) need protection against majoritarian tyranny—is a basic tenet of our constitutional system. Indeed, almost all of the cases we litigate at the Institute for Justice aim at shielding individuals against majoritarian or special interest excesses. It is where Guinier takes these premises that is profoundly troublesome.

Like most modern theorists, Guinier embraces an outcomes-oriented approach to civil rights. "The term 'anti-discrimination'," Guinier writes, "refers to more than the basic process of decision-making. It incorporates a result-oriented inquiry, in which roughly equal outcomes, not merely an apparently fair process, are the goal."[27]

In her book, *The Tyranny of the Majority,* Guinier distills a very complex and nuanced agenda into a simple principle. Based on an insight derived from her young son, Guinier would replace what she calls "winner-take-all majoritarianism" with the "principle of taking turns."[28]

Guinier's argument goes like this. In elections and the legislative arena, the majority always gets its way; as she puts it, "51 percent of the votes are . . . assured 100 percent of the power." In the rough and tumble of politics, the makeup of majorities shifts, allowing different groups to experience political satisfaction. But in Guinier's view, it doesn't work that way for racial minorities. "Simply put," she asserts, "racism excludes minorities from ever becoming part of the governing coalition, meaning that the white majority will be permanent."[29]

A powerful claim—and of course profoundly wrong. Whether measured by influence or outcomes, black and other racial minority politicians have wielded enormous clout in recent years. (Indeed, the Congressional Black Caucus was given veto power over Guinier's replacement, which it exercised to nix District of Columbia corporation counsel John Payton.) Yet her argument forms the central premise from which all Guinier's proposals flow.

To protect the interests of disfavored minorities, Guinier asserts, rules must be established that ensure "each group has a right to have its interests represented," and "each group has a right to have its interests satisfied a fair proportion of the time."[30]

Guinier applies those concepts in both the electoral and legislative contexts. In elections, she contends those groups have a right to "authentic" representation. Guinier explains: "Black representatives are authentic because they are elected by blacks and because they are descriptively similar to their constituents. In other words, they are politically, psychologically, and culturally black."[31] Black elected officials who were elected with substantial numbers of white votes, such as former Virginia governor L. Douglas Wilder, might not meet the standard of authenticity[32]; and Guinier ponders whether "descriptively black representatives who were also Republicans qualify as black representatives?"[33]

To facilitate authentic black representation, Guinier calls for elections by "cumulative voting": each voter has as many votes as there are open seats, and may cast them all for one candidate or for several. This supposedly would reflect intensity of voter preferences and increase authentic representation.[34]

In theory I have no objection to cumulative voting, though it likely would produce fewer Doug Wilders and more Gus Savages. What is objectionable is judicially imposed cumulative voting. The role of the courts under the Voting Rights Act is to ensure access to the ballot and to guarantee racially neutral rules—not to guarantee proportionate outcomes (as with racial gerrymandering) or to impose someone's idea of a perfect system of electoral representation.

But it is when Guinier transports her cumulative voting schemes to the legislative arena that her assault on "simple-minded notions of majority rule"[35] is most alarming. For Guinier even proportional and authentic representation in the electoral sphere is not enough: votes are "meaningless" and "wasted"—and therefore violative of the Voting Rights Act—unless the representatives who are elected can enact legislation.[36] The Voting Rights Act, she urges, "is not satisfied by proportionate election of members of a protected class," but instead adheres to a "principle of proportional power."[37] The appropriate remedy, Guinier suggests, is "proportionate interest representation," which provides that "at the legislative level, decisional rules other than either simple majority rule or one legislator/one vote may be required in order to ensure equal power."[38]

Under this system, instead of requiring majority votes to pass laws, different groups would "take turns" passing legislation through mechanisms variously described as "cumulati[ng]," "weight[ing]," or "plumping" votes.[39] In other words, legislators might be given as many votes as there were bills up for consideration, which they could cast singly or cumulatively. In a legislative body of 100 members, if there were ten bills up for consideration, 11 members could cumulate their votes and enact legislation that the other 89 opposed.

This innovation—which led me to label Guinier's proposals "breathtakingly radical"—would weaken an important constraint on government power. In a democracy, government may not exercise its powers unless at least a majority concurs. In this way, democracy provides an important structural check against tyranny. Under Guinier's system, that check would be removed. Far from curbing majoritarian tyranny, it would institute a regime of tyranny by the minority.

As disturbing as Guinier's proposed solutions are the premises on which they rely. Guinier's bogeyman—the monolithic "Majority"—simply does not exist. America is not divided into permanent, warring racial camps; it is not South Africa. By and large, blacks and whites share common principles, values, and aspirations. We have a political system that requires consensus, coalition, and compromise, a process that tends to heal racial divisions. The racial spoils system Guinier advocates to replace it would render her bleak vision a self-fulfilling prophesy.

More than any other parts of her writings, it was the portions urging that the Voting Rights Act be wielded to produce systemic changes to legislative processes[40] that convinced many readers—

apparently including the president—that Guinier's views were dangerously anti-democratic. But it was her belief that society is hopelessly and permanently divided along racial lines—therefore mandating a redistribution of political power along racial lines—that may have instigated the long-overdue process of rethinking the present course of the Voting Rights Act.

Those are the sorts of concerns that led the Supreme Court to place limits on racial gerrymandering in *Shaw v. Reno*. But the Court there addressed only the symptoms flowing from 25 years of judicial decisions that have taken the Voting Rights Act far from its intended course.

A more fundamental examination of voting rights jurisprudence may have started with the Court's 1994 decision in *Holder v. Hall*.[41] In that case, the black plaintiffs contended that the governing system of Bleckley County, Georgia, which always has consisted of a single commissioner elected at-large, constituted a "standard, practice, or procedure" that diluted minority voting strength in violation of section 2 of the Voting Rights Act. The plaintiffs charged that they would obtain greater representation if the single commissioner was replaced by a multimember board.

By a 5–4 vote, the Supreme Court rejected the claim. Because no standard "benchmark" existed for the size of county governing boards, the Court reasoned it could not measure whether the system diluted minority voting strength, thereby concluding that the size of an electoral district fell outside section 2's reach. For Justice Clarence Thomas, joined by Justice Antonin Scalia, the majority reached the right result but didn't go nearly far enough.[42] "I can no longer adhere to a reading of the Act that does not comport with the terms of the statute and that has produced such a disastrous misadventure in judicial policymaking," Thomas declared. Instead, he urged, the Court should construe the act to prohibit "only state enactments that limit citizens' access to the ballot."[43]

Thomas outlined two essential problems with the Court's voting rights jurisprudence. By broadly construing the term "standard, practice, or procedure" to encompass "dilution" of minority voting strength, "we have immersed the federal courts in a hopeless project of weighing questions of political theory."[44] Even worse, he continued, "we have devised a remedial mechanism that encourages federal courts to segregate voters into racially designated districts to ensure minority electoral success."[45]

Thomas proceeded to draw an explicit roadmap of the "destructive assumptions" underlying Voting Rights Act cases. The Court, he argued, has "converted the Act into a device for regulating, rationing, and apportioning political power among racial and ethnic groups." Such a mandate requires courts to choose among competing political theories "to determine which electoral systems provide the 'fairest' levels of representation or the most 'effective' or 'undiluted' votes to minorities," judgments that "courts are inherently ill-equipped to make."[46]

Even more alarming to Thomas than injecting the Court into political decisions is the premise, assumed by the vote dilution cases, that "race defines political interest." As Thomas explained, "We have acted on the implicit assumption that members of racial and ethnic groups must all think alike on matters of public policy and must have their own 'minority preferred' representatives holding seats in elected bodies if they are to be considered represented at all." These assumptions, Thomas argued, "should be repugnant to any nation that strives for the ideal of a color-blind Constitution"; and indeed, are similar to the reasoning that led to registering voters by race during the days of Jim Crow.[47]

Ultimately, Thomas concluded, the system leads to greater racial polarization. In a segregated voting system, "Neither group needs to draw on support from the other's constituency to win on election day." Moreover, the task of judicially reapportioning political power is invariably an expanding one. In a rueful reference to Lani Guinier, Thomas remarked, "We should not be surprised if voting rights advocates encourage us to 'revive our political imagination' . . . and to consider 'innovative and nontraditional remedies' for vote dilution."[48]

The only solution, Thomas urged, is for the Court to abandon the enterprise of political redistribution and return to the act's original purposes. "We would be mighty Platonic guardians indeed if Congress had granted us authority to determine the best form of local government for every county, city, village, and town in America," Thomas declared. "But under our constitutional system, this Court is not a centralized politburo appointed for life to dictate to the provinces. . . . We should be cautious in interpreting any Act of Congress to grant us power to make such determinations."[49]

Justice Thomas's eloquent opinion was a rare acknowledgment that the courts are the source of the voting rights conundrum in which we find ourselves today. And for better or worse, we must look to the courts to lead the way out of the thicket.

But something more is necessary. We should begin in earnest the discussion of whether the Voting Rights Act remains necessary. It does, after all, constitute a major federal intrusion into matters ordinarily left to local determination; hence its existence should be justified at every turn. Already the Supreme Court repeatedly is confronting whether race-conscious, results-oriented applications of the act violate more fundamental constitutional guarantees of equal protection of law. In the future, the Court surely will have to determine the due process and separation of powers implications of a Justice Department that simultaneously, and with few limits on its discretion, acts as lawmaker, law enforcer, and law adjudicator. The Court will also have to determine how far the national government can go, consistent with the constitutional doctrine of federalism, in displacing and second-guessing local decisionmaking.

If the act is repealed, it will not leave minorities helpless against voting rights violations. Both the Fourteenth and Fifteenth Amendments protect against government actions and policies that are based on race. What the repeal of the act would protect all of us against is social engineering schemes designed to promote ideological and partisan ends.

But whatever happens in the judicial and legislative arenas, the people must demand that our political system be deemed out of bounds for racial manipulation. The division of Americans along racial lines is too high a price to pay for perceived short-term political expediency. That means politicians and their supporters, whether white or black, Republican or Democrat, must be prepared to take their chances on the levelest possible playing field. Politics forces people to deal with one another; so much the better when racial separation is removed. When that competition begins to happen in earnest, perhaps we will be able to start anew the "dialogue" that so many in the civil rights establishment purport to want, but have done so much to thwart.

# 7. Bean-Counters and Quota Games: The Clinton Civil Rights Record

Quietly but ominously, the Clinton administration has set its civil rights policies on a radical course permeated by race-consciousness, brazenly breaking candidate Bill Clinton's "new Democrat" assurances that he would pursue a politics of moderation and healing.[1]

Despite displaying a moderate façade, President Clinton has done absolutely nothing to find common ground on race issues. Instead he has given over the entire federal civil rights apparatus to ideologues who cut their teeth in left-wing advocacy groups, unleashing them to pursue militant, in-your-face policies in areas touching the lives of every American.

Above it all, Clinton presides with benign indifference, reining in the zealots only when their more extreme mischief provokes public outrage. Otherwise he is satisfied to let them have their way, in what he mistakenly perceives to be a low-cost appeasement of those who dwell at his party's left boundary.

For civil rights activists marginalized during the Reagan and Bush years, Clinton's approach is nirvana. And the activists are flexing their newfound muscle with partisan vengeance. Twelve years of "neglect" and "active hostility to civil rights progress," proclaims Justice Department civil rights chief Deval Patrick, "can be summed up in one word: Republicans."[2]

But for ordinary Americans of all colors, the brave new world is not so joyful. For the nation's already simmering race relations, the administration's policies are incendiary. And they leave tragically unaddressed serious problems that are fomenting severe divisions in our society.

As columnist Dorothy Gilliam observed during the 1992 presidential campaign, "none of the leading contenders has chosen or been forced to deal with civil rights matters in the way candidates have

97

had to in every election since 1944."[3] George Bush neutralized himself by signing the Civil Rights Act of 1991, which previously he had denounced as a quota bill. Clinton seized upon Bush's predicament to recapture Democrats alienated by the party's support for race preferences and other social welfare programs. Clinton talked tough about welfare and middle class virtues. He responded to one critic: "If trying to restore the middle class in this country is a code word for racism, we are in deep trouble. We might as well fold our tent and go home."[4]

For the most part, candidate Clinton's rhetoric was soothing and conciliatory on race issues: "America needs to restore the old spirit of partnership, of optimism, of renewed dedication to common efforts," he declared.[5] But it was Clinton's high-profile attack on rap singer Sister Souljah for her provocation of violence against whites that made believers among mainstream Democrats that Clinton would not be a hostage to extremists on race issues.

After the election, Clinton righteously rebuffed demands for more appointments of women and minorities to his cabinet, denouncing his critics as "bean counters" who were "playing quota games."[6] And when his first nominee for assistant attorney general for civil rights, former NAACP Legal Defense Fund lawyer Lani Guinier, was assailed for her radical views, Clinton withdrew the nomination.

All this gave genuine new Democrats cause for optimism. President Clinton's withdrawal of the Guinier nomination, proclaimed Will Marshall, president of the centrist Progressive Policy Institute, "reaffirms the stance he took during the campaign, which was unwavering support for civil rights . . ., but not support for quotas, group rights, or special preferences."[7]

But it turned out Guinier was no aberration, for Clinton's appointees to virtually every civil rights post bear the same activist pedigrees. The list reads like a roll call of establishment civil rights groups. Deval Patrick worked with Guinier at the NAACP Legal Defense Fund. Patrick plucked Kerry Scanlon from the Legal Defense Fund's ranks for one deputy position, and for another chose Isabelle Pinzler, director of the American Civil Liberties Union's Women's Rights Project.

At the Equal Employment Opportunity Commission (EEOC), Clinton appointed as chairman former Air Force counsel Gilbert Casellas, who previously worked for the Puerto Rican Legal Defense and Education Fund. The other two new commissioners are Paul Igasaki, who served as executive director of the Asian Law Caucus; and Paul Miller, formerly litigation director for the Western Law Center for Disability Rights. The commission's legal counsel, Ellen Vargyas, worked for the National Women's Law Center.

At the Department of Education, Clinton named as assistant secretary for civil rights Norma Cantu, regional counsel for the Mexican-American Legal Defense and Education Fund. Roberta Achtenberg, assistant secretary for fair housing and equal opportunity at the Department of Housing and Urban Development, worked as executive director of the National Center for Lesbian Rights. And Clinton elevated as chairperson of the U.S. Commission on Civil Rights long-time commissioner Mary Frances Berry, who came to national attention in 1985 when she opined that "civil rights laws were not passed to give civil rights to all Americans," but only to give them to "disfavored groups" such as "blacks, Hispanics, and women."[8]

These appointments mark a historical milestone: for the first time, an entire area of federal policy—in this case civil rights—has been handed over wholesale to a special interest lobby. They are operating out of new offices, but advancing the same agendas—with the federal government's mighty civil rights arsenal now at their disposal.

Throughout the administration, the touchstone for political appointments has been precisely the racial and gender parity candidate Clinton disparaged. Ironically, the bean-counting stymied civil rights law enforcement by delaying key appointments while the desired diversity mix was found. Limiting serious consideration of attorney general candidates to women left the Justice Department rudderless for months until finally third-choice Janet Reno was nominated. The Civil Rights Division was without a chief for more than a year as the administration searched for a black candidate rather than elevate one of the white career deputies.

In Mississippi, the Clinton administration left its candidate for United States Attorney for the Northern District twisting in the wind for two years before dumping him on racial grounds in favor of a manifestly less-qualified choice. The original pick, Josh Bogen, was a staunch Democrat with strong civil rights credentials who had argued hundreds of cases. Bogen was passed over in favor of Buck Buchanan, a junior prosecutor who had never handled a major case and ranked 14th in seniority in an office of 16. But Bogen is white and Buchanan is black. In the meantime, conceded one senior administration official, "The politics of this has fused to gridlock."[9]

But the most perverse display of bean-counting involved the EEOC, where the Clinton administration left the chairmanship vacant for 21 months as it searched for a nominee who, as the *Washington Post* described it, was "not just Hispanic," but specifically of "Puerto Rican descent." This "caricature of equal employment opportunity policy," the *Post* editorialized, comes "perilously close to institutionalizing some of the very distinctions as to ethnicity, race, gender and all the rest" that the commission is supposed to combat.[10] Meanwhile, as Ronald Brownstein of the *Los Angeles Times* reported, the delay "left the agency foundering as it struggles to dig out from a massive backlog of more than 80,000 pending discrimination complaints."[11]

Having survived the bean count, chairman Casellas presides over an agency that is weighing such lofty questions as whether infertility, obesity, and nicotine addiction qualify for protection under the Americans with Disabilities Act. But even more pressing is a command from liberals on Capitol Hill that Casellas purge from the agency anyone who deviates from the new political correctness. In an October 6, 1994, letter, Sen. Paul Simon reminded Casellas about

> the agreement you made to me during your confirmation hearing. I had asked that as the new Chairman, you send to me a letter within six months regarding those in the agency who do not believe in the mission of the EEOC . . . [who] should be transferred to the Pentagon or someplace else.[12]

If the purge victims turn out to be white males, they may find their problems only beginning if they are moved to the Pentagon. On August 10, 1994, Undersecretary of Defense Edwin Dorn issued a memorandum implementing Secretary William J. Perry's call for "vigorous action" to increase the number of "women, minorities and persons with disabilities . . . among the Department's civilian managers." Remarking that "progress in this area comes one job at a time," Dorn directed that "I need to be consulted whenever you are confronting the possibility that any excepted position, or any career position at GS-15 level and higher, is likely to be filled by a candidate who will not enhance . . . diversity." If this mechanism failed, Dorn warned, "we will need to employ a more formal approach involving goals, timetables and controls on hiring deci-sions."[13]

Dorn's message was none too subtle. "As a white male, I can kiss my future goodbye," complained one GS-14 Defense Department employee to the *Washington Post.* "I am keeping Dorn's memo handy [in case] for some unexpected reason I do apply for advancement. It should serve as excellent prima facie evidence of discrimination due to race."[14]

The administration's bean-counting obsession is so pervasive that hardly a personnel decision is made without considering "diversity" consequences. Perhaps most revealing was the memorandum recently reprinted in *Washington Monthly* from Roger Kennedy, National Park Service director, to some subordinates:

> Surely, we must be able to find a use for a Swahili-speaking person who has Peace Corps experience, is a cum laude in English from Harvard and has a biological background in data manipulation. . . . Unfortunately, Mr. Trevor is white, which is too bad.[15]

But "diversity" within the Clinton administration is not just about numbers, it is also about political correctness. In January 1994, HUD established "cultural diversity" performance standards for manag-ers and supervisors, giving them points on their evaluations if they "speak favorably about minorities, women, persons with disabilities and others of diverse backgrounds"; "participate as an active mem-ber of minority, feminist or other cultural organizations"; and "par-ticipate in EEO and Cultural Diversity activities outside of HUD."

HUD's directives were condemned by the Senior Executive Asso-ciation as violations of freedom of speech and association. "While the law requires that employees not discriminate for or against any-one on the basis of race, color, religion, sex, [or] national origin," the association wrote HUD's Achtenberg, "it does not, in fact, require that career executives become advocates for particular groups and adopt their agendas."[16] An apt complaint, but not one likely to sway those who see no difference between enforcing the law and advancing an agenda.

Far more significant than the quota regime installed within the federal government are the social engineering policies imposed upon the rest of us under the guise of civil rights.

Though civil rights policy is diffused among many agencies, the fulcrum is the Justice Department's Civil Rights Division, where Deval Patrick rapidly shed any pretense of impartial law enforcement in favor of unbridled ideological activism.

Both Patrick and Attorney General Janet Reno projected moderate images on race issues at their confirmation hearings. Reno assured Senator Hank Brown (R-Colo.) that "Quotas shouldn't be used anywhere, sir." Patrick was even more demure. A racial quota, meaning "a particular number which is both a ceiling and a floor," is "against the law," responded Patrick to a query from Sen. Strom Thurmond (R-S.C.). But even "affirmative action," which is "something different from that"—namely, "goals and timetables" that "starts with recruitment and training"—"has to be reserved for limited circumstances, and has to be flexible," Patrick testified. "And I understand that to be the law of the land and part of the responsibility of the division in abiding [by] the law of the land, sir."[17]

Patrick's fidelity to the law lasted less than five months. The vehicle Patrick chose to signal a new direction was *United States v. Board of Education of Piscataway*, a New Jersey reverse discrimination case the Justice Department won on behalf of white schoolteacher Sharon Taxman, who was fired during a reduction-in-force to retain a black teacher with equal seniority. The school board previously resolved such matters with a coin flip, but this time decided by race to preserve "diversity." The case was brought by the Bush administration but prosecuted by the Reno Justice Department before Patrick's arrival.

Federal courts have allowed the limited use of race only to remedy an employer's past discrimination or gross statistical disparities. In this case, neither justification was availing since the school board had an exemplary record of minority hiring. Judge Maryann Trump Barry refused to accept the board's "diversity" rationale because it would allow "boundless" race preferences—precisely what advocates of "affirmative action" desire—and she struck down Piscataway's blatant act of discrimination.[18]

But this victory Patrick and company could not abide. At first, they inclined toward merely sitting out the appeal, forcing Taxman to defend the decision alone in the Third Circuit Court of Appeals. But Patrick's deputy, Kerry Scanlon, pressed for a bolder approach: switch sides altogether.

Scanlon prevailed, and Patrick himself signed the motion to realign the United States with the party it had just successfully prosecuted for violating the Civil Rights Act of 1964. Patrick thumbed his nose at a long series of Supreme Court decisions (see Chapter 4), declaring in his motion that the trial court applied "an unduly narrow interpretation of the permissible bases for affirmative action."

Patrick and Scanlon miscalculated the public outcry and soon were backpedaling. Patrick declared at a news conference that the case was "unique and narrow," because it involved "two teachers who were equally qualified and identical in seniority." But still he defended the underlying logic, insisting that "the concept of faculty diversity does not favor one race over another." Regardless of how narrow the facts of this particular case, if courts were to accept "diversity" as a permissible justification for racial preferences, it would obliterate any meaningful limitation on such policies.

Patrick can implement much of his agenda without filing a single lawsuit. When the Justice Department knocks at a door and threatens to unleash its vast litigation arsenal, rational people often turn compliant. Hence Patrick and others who possess civil rights law enforcement authority are not ultimately bounded so much by what a court might approve, but only by what a school board or employer or elected official might "voluntarily" agree to do.

A classic example involved Fullerton, California, on whose doors Patrick knocked in spring 1995, bearing a charge of employment discrimination in one hand and an invitation to surrender in the other.[19] If Fullerton acquiesced, it would have to submit to quota hiring for its police and fire departments and a host of other race-conscious mandates, even as it was laying off employees. If it refused, it would have to bear massive costs to defend itself: nearby Torrance already had spent over $1 million in 21 months of litigation against a similar Justice Department lawsuit. Either way, the city loses.

Fullerton's mayor, Julie Sa, insisted the city was guilty of no wrongdoing and was aware of no individual claims of discrimination. The Justice Department wanted the city to produce a 44.3 percent minority applicant pool, including 9.1 percent blacks, in a city whose minority population is 37 percent minority and 1.9 percent black. Its statistical analysis seemed to draw more from the entire Los Angeles metropolitan area, which is more heavily minority than Fullerton, rather than from Orange County, which is less so. Fullerton is in Orange County, about 22 miles from the city of Los Angeles.

Patrick demanded that the city sign a consent decree obligating it to actively recruit in minority-targeted media and other outlets designed to increase minority hiring. Failure to achieve racial parity would trigger Justice Department scrutiny. The city also had to hire on a priority basis minorities who applied (or felt discouraged from applying) for entry-level police and fire positions since 1985, and provide back pay and benefits.

The power to induce not-so-voluntary settlement agreements opens up new vistas for those invested with broad law enforcement powers, so that what is today the fevered figment of an ideologue's imagination may be tomorrow's real-world nightmare. For Chevy Chase Savings & Loan, that future arrived on August 22, 1994, when Reno and Patrick announced a consent decree that the financial institution signed to avoid prosecution for lending discrimination. The Justice Department produced no evidence that Chevy Chase discriminated in loan approvals. Rather, it charged the savings & loan had insufficient branch offices in certain minority census tracts, which in Reno's and Patrick's eyes amounted to illegally "shunning" a "community."

Under the unprecedented settlement, Chevy Chase agreed not only to open new branches, but also to adopt hiring quotas, approve loans for blacks at below-market rates, provide grants to cover down payments, and advertise in minority-owned media outlets, including "at least 960 column inches" of advertisements in black-targeted newspapers.[20]

As Cornell law professor Jonathan Macey charges, "The government's willingness to proceed with litigation in the absence of evidence of discrimination" is "scandalous in a nation that purports to be governed by a rule of law."[21] Instead of prosecuting banks that actually discriminate—or dealing with underlying problems that discourage banks from opening offices in low-income areas—Patrick seems determined to pursue high-profile cases that resemble naked extortion more than civil rights law enforcement.

Rather than fight overwhelming odds, the Mortgage Banking Association, the nation's largest mortgage lending association, engaged in preemptive capitulation. Roberta Achtenberg announced in September 1994 an agreement with the association that called upon members to bolster minority lending, advertise in minority media outlets, and "encourage development of a workforce that reflects the cultural, racial and ethnic diversity of the lenders' market."[22]

Meanwhile, new Clinton regulations make Patrick's job easier by demanding racial identification from applicants for consumer or business loans under $1 million. And in case the federal civil rights arsenal is inadequate to the task, Patrick and deputy Scanlon are urging private-sector lawyers to take up litigation. "You can make money on fair housing cases," Scanlon told a lawyer group.[23]

Like his former colleague Lani Guinier, Patrick is also determined to wield the Voting Rights Act to redistribute political power. Condemning the Supreme Court's 1993 *Shaw v. Reno* decision striking down racially gerrymandered election districts as "alternately naive and venal," Patrick has organized a seven-member team within the Civil Rights Division to defend against "every single challenge" to such districts.[24] The Justice Department filed briefs in the Supreme Court defending blatant racially gerrymandered congressional districts in Georgia and Louisiana.

The problem with Patrick's voting rights approach is that it substitutes policy objectives (defending racial gerrymandering) for objective law enforcement (determining on a case-by-case basis whether such districts accord with the law). But it typifies the ideological approach to civil rights law enforcement that pervades the Clinton administration. Indeed, the Justice Department's extensive resources in the voting rights area supplement a half-million-dollar grant awarded by the Carnegie Foundation to the Lawyers' Committee for Civil Rights for same purpose—making it hard to tell the special interest groups from the law enforcement agencies.

Companies subject to heavy federal regulation are easy prey to social engineering schemes, perhaps none so susceptible as those who depend on Federal Communications Commission licenses for their existence. In January 1994, the FCC issued new rules imposing heavy fines on broadcasters for failure to meet explicit quotas for hiring minorities and women.[25]

And in what the *New York Times* called the "biggest affirmative-action program in decades," the FCC voted to set aside half of 2,000 licenses for wireless "personal communications services" (such as portable phones and pagers) for firms owned by minority individuals and women, and to provide licenses for such companies at up to 60 percent below market value. One analyst valued the benefits at half a billion dollars.

Like all set-asides, the FCC program is welfare for the wealthy. It is also prime for abuse: as the *Times* reports, the 50 percent minority ownership threshold means that "a company could still qualify for the full range of preferences even if huge corporate investors acquired 75 percent of the equity and 49.9 percent of the voting stock."[26] Moreover, the program cannot possibly satisfy constitutional requirements: since the licenses involve new communications technologies, by definition there can be no "past discrimination" to justify racial or gender preferences of any sort.

But constitutional constraints are no impediment to the Clinton civil rights regime. In 1994, HUD launched a Fair Housing Act investigation against three Berkeley residents for opposing a planned homeless shelter in their neighborhood, threatening each with fines up to $100,000 and a year in jail if they did not turn over all their records, including lists of their coalition's members. HUD subsequently disclosed similar investigations around the country, aimed at suppressing what Heather MacDonald, writing in the *Wall Street Journal*, described as "textbook examples of petitioning the government for a redress of grievances."[27]

After widespread publicity, HUD's Achtenberg backed down, conceding that the "Berkeley citizens acted within their First Amendment, free-speech rights." She pledged that "every attempt is being made to ensure that HUD's inquiries . . . do not have a chilling effect on political activity or the exercise of free speech." But, warned Achtenberg, "We can anticipate more cases of this kind."[28]

The Education Department's Norma Cantu was similarly red-faced when it was disclosed that her Office of Civil Rights was investigating Ohio's high school proficiency examinations—even after a federal court ruled the tests were not racially biased. The 2.6 percent of graduating seniors who failed the exam—about one-third of whom were black—were offered a 10-hour summer remediation course and another chance to pass. But the racially disproportionate results were intolerable to Cantu, who backed down only when challenged by Rep. Bill Goodling (R-Pa.) and 14 other members of Congress.[29]

The Department has persisted, however, in its support for race-exclusive college scholarships. Reversing a Bush administration policy emphasizing disadvantage over race, Education Secretary Richard Riley embraced race-based scholarships, calling them "a valuable tool for providing equal opportunity and for enhancing a diverse educational environment."[30] The Department's efforts to defend the constitutionality of such programs were rebuffed, however, when the U.S. Supreme Court refused to review the federal appeals court decision striking down the University of Maryland's race-based scholarship program (see Chapter 5).

The major effect of embracing race rather than disadvantage in college scholarships—conferring benefits on the offspring of Jesse Jackson and members of the Congressional Black Caucus rather than on the children of Anacostia—seems to have escaped the Clinton administration. But the policy exemplifies Clinton's approach to civil rights: redistributing benefits and opportunities on the basis of race, rather than engaging in any meaningful effort to develop common-ground solutions to the problems facing society's most disadvantaged members. While the Clinton administration pursues racial entitlements, it has fiercely resisted such efforts to empower low-income people as school choice, tenant management of public housing, and repeal of the Davis-Bacon Act, a racist law enacted in 1931 that prevents many low-skilled workers from entering the construction trades.

The courts have rejected the Clinton administration's views on civil rights in virtually every major case—from race-based scholarships, to minority set-asides, employment preferences, racial gerrymandering, and desegregation. Yet the administration still has tremendous discretion, through its policies and law-enforcement powers, to push its race-conscious agenda.

In early 1995, following the election of a Republican Congress, Clinton pledged to review federal affirmative action programs to root out those that do not work, a process hastened by the Supreme Court's *Adarand* ruling later that year calling into question most federal race preference programs (see Chapter 4). Instead the president delivered only superficial pablum, pledging to "mend, not end" race-based affirmative action. Clinton's nebulous standards promised to provide a figleaf for virtually all the existing racial preference programs. What's more, Clinton clearly missed the point when he said he would examine preference programs to see if they "work": if they discriminate, they do not work. As has so often been the case with this president, he is searching for a third position on an issue on which there really are only two sides: either the government will be allowed to discriminate, or it will not. Under Clinton, despite the rhetoric, clearly it will.

This policy choice, a betrayal of both the party's liberal heritage and its more recent centrist pretensions, spells serious problems both for Clinton specifically and for Democrats generally. The issue of racial preferences, which Clinton neatly sidestepped in 1992, will not stay buried for long. And the positions Clinton has taken will not be popular with mainstream voters. Half of those who voted for Clinton oppose race preferences.[31] And as Paul M. Sniderman and Thomas Piazza found in their polling on racial attitudes,

> The feelings of ordinary Americans on questions of race run strong. The issue of race matters deeply to them, and they know where they stand on it. Race is a red-flag issue, and even if their interest in public affairs is minimal and sporadic, even if they find discussions of the day arid and boring, the issue of race hits home, and their response to it is immediate, emotional, visceral.[32]

A microcosm of how far the Clinton administration's policies have strayed from the popular consensus on civil rights is the Piscataway case. *USA Today* put the question to the public: where a school district has increased the percentage of minority teachers through affirmative action and now is faced with layoffs, and where a white and black teacher are equally qualified, how should the decision be made? Seventy-three percent thought the school district should flip a coin; only three percent agreed with the school district's position that the white teacher should be laid off.[33] The columnist Charles Krauthammer aptly summarizes the political dynamics:

> After 20 years it has simply become impossible to suppress by intimidation the deeply held feeling of a vast majority of Americans that our tangled system of racial preferences is fundamentally un-American, destructive and actually poisonous to race relations. Because when the Department of Justice (sic) blandly defends the racially motivated firing of a teacher in the name of "a policy of equal educational opportunity," our threshold for Orwellian doublethink has finally been breached.[34]

Democrats in the 1960s stood firmly for the principle of equal opportunity. Will they cast off the demagogues that have pried them away from that principle, or continue down the road of racially divisive policies? There is a strong current within the Democratic Party that believes in the liberal ideal of equality under law. This is one issue on which principle and expediency coincide. If Democrats renounce racial preferences and embrace equal opportunity, they will reclaim the political center while reclaiming the moral high ground on civil rights. But their president has spurned this impulse, professing mainstream Democratic principles while betraying them.

Of far greater consequence than this president's political prognosis, however, is the future of race relations in America. The Clinton administration has been the most quota-driven in history. Stoking the fires of racial backlash and division is too high a price to pay for appeasing the party's left wing. The Democrats, who did so much to promote a civil rights vision that treats people not as members of groups but as individuals, should return to the principles they once cherished.

# 8. The Republican Abdication

There I sat for the first time in the inner sanctum of the White House, the president flanking me on my right. I had been designated spokesman for the groups present in the room who opposed a bill sponsored by Sen. Edward Kennedy (D-Mass.) and then-Rep. Augustus Hawkins (D-Calif.) to overturn several Supreme Court civil rights decisions. I was so intensely focused on my mission that when I was asked that evening to describe the room and surroundings in which the meeting took place, I could not remember a single detail.

In a manner befitting the internal schizophrenia of the Bush administration, the meeting encompassed disparate elements: liberal feminists and conservative activists. The White House had hastily arranged three meetings between interest groups and the president to figure out what to do about the civil rights decisions and the Democrats' bill. One meeting included black leaders, another Hispanics, leaving only one for the feminists and conservatives to combine in cacophonous discord.

That these meetings ever took place was typical of a Republican disconnect on civil rights issues that has spanned the better part of four decades. The Supreme Court rulings at issue were the fruit of 10 years of appointments intended to rein in the kind of unreconstructed judicial activism that had produced forced busing, quotas, and racial gerrymandering. At the apex of the judicial counterrevolution was the 1989 *Wards Cove* decision, which harmonized the implementation of the Civil Rights Act of 1964 with the intent of its framers and cooled considerably the quota engines (see Chapter 4). It was a decision all Republicans should have cheered as a triumph of the principles of fairness and equal opportunity.

Because *Wards Cove* addressed not merely the symptoms but the core premise of civil rights revisionism—that statistical disparities demonstrate discrimination—I had urged conservatives and the business community to circle the wagons around it. Not only were the rulings correct and important, but also the political terrain seemed to have shifted, quietly yet significantly. By framing the issue as racial quotas vs. fundamental fairness, advocates of a colorblind society for the first time were able to seize from the civil rights establishment the moral high ground.

The civil rights groups reacted to the decisions with predictable hysteria, accusing the Supreme Court of turning back the clock on civil rights. Although the Kennedy/Hawkins bill aimed at overturning several civil rights rulings, the liberals recognized that *Wards Cove* was crucial. They proposed to shift the burden of proof to employers accused of discrimination on the basis of statistics, and to make the "business necessity" justification nearly impossible to establish. It was a complex argument, and it resonated little with mainstream blacks. When the NAACP's then-executive director Benjamin Hooks called for a mass march on Washington to protest the Supreme Court rulings, the turnout was so small he was forced to downsize the event to a "silent vigil."[1]

But in the face of this historic opportunity to shift the terms of the debate, the reflexive Republican instinct was to retreat. Even before the Democrats had formulated a strategy, Rep. Tom Campbell (R-Calif.) introduced legislation to overturn *Wards Cove*. President Bush indulged his patrician, noblesse oblige predilections, announcing at the meeting with black civil rights leaders on May 14, 1990, that he "would like to sign a civil rights bill," and had only "minimal" differences with the Kennedy-Hawkins proposal.[2]

Realizing we had little time to change the president's mind, we mounted a furious counteroffensive. The battle over policy direction on civil rights—and ultimately for the soul of the Republican Party— was waged both inside and outside the White House.[3] Joined by Bob Woodson of the National Center for Neighborhood Enterprise and others, I argued that Bush should resist such legislation and instead commit himself to a positive alternative civil rights program grounded in individual empowerment.[4] Meanwhile, key administration officials including White House counsel C. Boyden Gray and EEOC vice-chair Ricky Silberman urged Bush to stand firm against the Kennedy-Hawkins bill.[5]

The decision was announced a few days later at a sunny Rose Garden gathering that was packed with denizens of the civil rights establishment, eagerly awaiting word that Bush would endorse their agenda. They were disappointed. Bush instead outlined three prerequisites for a civil rights bill: it must not require or encourage quotas, it must not be so complex as to constitute a make-work bill for lawyers, and it must not overturn the due-process principle of innocent until proven guilty.[6] The Kennedy-Hawkins proposal violated all three principles.

The three principles set forth by the president were simple and compelling—in stark contrast to the complex explanations advanced by the bill's proponents. Although the bill was passed by the Democrat-controlled Congress, there were enough votes to sustain a veto. The White House negotiated intensely with the civil rights establishment, but Bush stood firm. Rejecting further moves down the road to quotas, Bush outlined in his veto message a different vision of civil rights:

> In order to address these problems, attention must be given to measures that promote accountability and parental choice in the schools; that strengthen the fight against violent criminals and drug dealers in our inner cities; and that help to combat poverty and inadequate housing. We need initiatives that will empower individual Americans and enable them to reclaim control of their lives, thus helping to make our country's promise of opportunity a reality for all. Enactment of such in initiatives ... will achieve real advances for the cause of equal opportunity.[7]

After an unsuccessful attempt to override the veto, the Democrats' bill was introduced again the following year. Though the administration remained internally divided, Bush appeared resolute, denouncing the measure as a "quota bill."[8] But the battle this time was interrupted by the resignation of Justice Thurgood Marshall and the nomination of federal judge Clarence Thomas to the U.S. Supreme Court. Even though the civil rights groups bitterly opposed Thomas, blacks supported confirmation by a three-to-one margin, demonstrating the chasm between civil rights leaders and their purported constituents.[9]

But after Thomas was confirmed, the White House seemed to lose its stomach for the battle. Within weeks, the White House agreed to a bill that violated all three of the principles Bush had set forth. The signing ceremony was attended by the same establishment civil rights figures who had fought the administration on both civil rights and the Thomas nomination, while the administration's loyal allies were left to lick the wounds of betrayal.

Along with its principles, the Bush administration jettisoned any meaningful effort to fashion a coherent, forward-looking approach to civil rights. With its capitulation on the quota bill, the Bush administration fumbled away not only a winning political issue, but also any chance to refashion the debate in a positive way.

This experience with the 1991 civil rights bill epitomizes the disastrous Republican approach toward civil rights issues. However misguided the civil rights policies of the Democrats, the Republican record has been worse. Thirty years of not-so-benign Republican neglect have left a dangerous civil rights orthodoxy unchallenged and the principles underlying the American civil rights vision unchampioned.

Alone among major areas of public policy, civil rights issues over the years have virtually been ceded to Democrats by Republicans and to liberals by conservatives. There have been many opportunities over the past three decades for Republicans to attach themselves firmly to the traditional consensus on civil rights. But every such opportunity has passed without Republicans seizing it. Instead, the Republican reaction (and always it has been a reaction rather than an initiative) has typically consisted of two approaches: either acquiescing in the Democrats' civil rights agenda, or merely opposing that agenda without offering a credible response. The first approach is unsatisfying, for it means that destructive policies are conferred the imprimatur of bipartisan consensus, and that principles of individualism and equal opportunity are removed from the debate. The second approach exposes Republicans and conservatives to justifiable charges of being anti-civil rights.

The situation was not always so, for before 1964 the Republican party had a noble civil rights pedigree that traced back to the party's roots in the abolitionist movement. From its creation in 1854, the Republican party embraced a philosophy of freedom and empowerment. For the next 75 years, Republicans were the champions of civil rights, and blacks overwhelmingly voted Republican.[10]

Starting with the New Deal, blacks began voting Democratic for economic reasons, and over time Republican interest in civil rights issues dwindled in favor of "states' rights."[11] By the late 1960s, the metamorphosis was complete with the adoption by the GOP of the "Southern strategy" to realign the electorate. As Republican strategist Kevin Phillips argued in 1969, "Obviously, the GOP can build a winning coalition without Negro votes."[12]

For being on the wrong side of civil rights in the mid-1960s, Republicans have ever since tried to atone, yet in ways not always constructive. Paralyzed by guilt, they have abetted civil rights policies that profoundly contradict supposed Republican principles.

Indeed, despite its rhetoric against forced busing and quotas, it was the Nixon Administration that "invented and consolidated the machinery that would nationally enforce . . . affirmative action," observes Hugh Davis Graham.[13] Nixon transformed affirmative action into a euphemism for quotas by imposing race-based "goals and timetables" on private contractors through the so-called "Philadelphia Plan" and the Office of Federal Contract Compliance.[14] Nixon also created the Office of Minority Business Enterprise and inaugurated minority contract set-asides.[15] Under Nixon, the EEOC grew from a staff of 359 and budget of $13.2 million in 1968 to a staff of 1,640 and a budget of $29.5 million in 1972. Funding for federal minority set-asides likewise grew from $8.2 million in fiscal year 1972 to $242.2 million in fiscal 1974—nearly a 3,000 percent increase.[16]

As Shelby Steele observes, "Racial quotas came in during the Nixon administration, not because Republicans believed in them, but because they lacked the moral authority to resist them."[17] At nearly every subsequent juncture, Republicans have seemed spineless in resisting policies that violate core principles of individualism and freedom. Even the Reagan administration, which launched a counteroffensive in the courts to curb the excesses of the liberal civil rights agenda, acquiesced legislatively in much the same agenda. And with the mere stroke of a pen, Reagan could have erased Executive Order 11246, the coercive catalyst for private sector reverse discrimination (see Chapter 4)—but over eight years failed to do so. The Bush administration arrived at the crucial crossroads in the battle over the Civil Rights Act of 1991, and repeated the disastrous errors of its Republican predecessors.

For all the costs entailed in abandoning their principles, the Republicans have not reaped dividends among black voters at the polls. Despite having signed the Civil Rights Act of 1991, George Bush's percentage of the black vote actually *decreased* to 11 percent in 1992 from 12 percent four years earlier—the same proportion Ronald Reagan received in 1980. The Republican share of Hispanic voters also declined, from 37 percent in 1984 to 30 percent in 1988 and 25 percent in 1992.

Nor is the Republican party portraying itself effectively as the party of opportunity for low-income voters. Remarkably, Ronald Reagan in 1984 attracted 45 percent of voters with incomes under $15,000, who constitute 14 percent of the electorate. By 1988 that figure had declined to 37 percent and in 1992 the Republican share plummeted to 23 percent.[18]

What should be especially distressing to Republicans in this regard is that while a plurality of blacks (33 percent) describe themselves as conservative rather than moderate or liberal, only 5 percent identify themselves as Republicans.[19] The difference between these two figures suggests an enormous credibility gap the Republicans have built for themselves. Imagine the impact if all blacks who described themselves as conservative also voted Republican: that likely would ensure not only continued GOP control of Congress, but the recapturing of the presidency as well. But in fact the Republicans seem to be moving in the opposite direction in narrowing rather than broadening their base.

They cannot sustain that direction for long. The percentage of the American population that is white declined from 83.3 percent in 1970 to 75.3 percent in 1990[20]—and is steadily shrinking. A party that relies on racially gerrymandered congressional districts and an ever-dwindling ethnic base places itself in serious jeopardy. As it approaches the 21st century, the challenge facing the Republican party is clear: expand its base, or shrivel and eventually die.

So what should Republicans do? For most Republicans it is counterintuitive that the party can oppose racial preferences and still improve its ability to attract minority voters, but evidence suggests this is true. Certainly the converse is not true: where Republicans have embraced race-conscious policies, they have not induced black voters to support Republicans. Such efforts are profoundly patronizing: if faced with a choice between real supporters and pretend supporters of preferences, voters who care about such policies will choose the real thing every time.

But the fact is that few minority voters care much about such policies. Polls consistently find that blacks are about evenly divided over racial preferences.[21] Moreover, among those who oppose ending racial preferences, less than half are strongly opposed.[22]

Instead, Republicans should do something in the area of civil rights that is novel for them: stand firmly and unapologetically

116

behind their principles, and reach out to potential constituencies they typically have ignored. This strategy entails making common cause on issues where Republican principles overlap with the interests of minority individuals. The opportunity to do so is greater than ever. "With a slow but steady shift in their interests from civil rights to economics," asserts Matthew Rees, author of the definitive study on blacks and the Republican party, "blacks have begun to make themselves available to the Republican party. The question now is whether or not the Republican party is going to make itself once again available to blacks."[23]

The challenge is stiff one—overcoming generations of well-earned cynicism toward Republicans—and it means that Republicans will have to venture into rarely traversed terrain. "If Republican candidates were willing to campaign in black churches," suggests Rees, "they would be almost assured of increasing their level of black support."[24] Likewise, traditional Republican objectives such as school choice, safe streets, low taxes, and economic development appeal to voters across the racial spectrum.

Republicans can expand their appeal to low-income people by promoting empowerment policies that give individuals a personal stake in free enterprise and individual initiative (see Chapter 10). School vouchers, tenant management of public housing, meaningful welfare reform, and strong crime prevention programs can resonate intensely among low-income voters. It will take some time to overcome decades of well-earned distrust, but Republicans will continue to fare abysmally if they continue to ignore minority voters.

Since Republicans have been stumbling around for so long on civil rights issues, why should now be any different? Indeed, evidence suggests that Republicans will continue their passivity on civil rights, even when presented with stellar political opportunities. In July 1995, despite having developed a principled bill to curb the federal government's power to discriminate, congressional Republicans got cold feet and allowed President Clinton to announce his own civil rights approach first and therefore to define the terms of the debate.

Republicans may yet have the chance to display resolve. The Equal Opportunity Act, introduced in summer 1995 by Senate Majority Leader Robert Dole (R-Kans.) and Rep. Charles Canady (R-Fla.), seized the moral high ground by seeking to make the federal government colorblind and gender-neutral. As a practical matter, Republicans no longer will be able to avoid taking a stand on the question of racial preferences. Voter initiatives and proposed legislation abound at the state and federal levels. Republican tendencies to compromise on these issues may be tempered by the fact that on one central question, no middle-ground position exists: either the government should have the power to discriminate or it should not. For principled (or politically sensible) Republicans, this question should present little difficulty.

Perhaps more significant in the willingness of Republicans finally to confront these issues is the passing of the torch to a new generation of leadership. Most of the new conservative and Republican leaders in the public policy arena are too young to recall the era of state-sanctioned segregation—or, more significant, to carry any baggage for opposing civil rights measures in the 1960s. To the contrary, the only state-imposed discrimination my generation has witnessed is *reverse* discrimination. We oppose it for the same reasons, and I hope with much of the same passion, as those who sought an end to discrimination a generation ago.

Where the Republicans could go wrong—badly wrong—on this issue is by succumbing to their persistent impulse to "compromise." On the issue of government's power to discriminate, there is no middle ground: either it can discriminate or it cannot. If Republicans give in to demands that they acquiesce in some exception to the principle of nondiscrimination, they will have sacrificed a historic opportunity to get the government out of the business of discrimination once and for all, and thereby to begin anew the process of racial healing. The party will have lost as well the chance to align itself solidly with a broad and multiracial consensus against racial preferences.

But beyond their fidelity to the principle of nondiscrimination, Republicans will ultimately be judged by the effort and ingenuity they invest in expanding opportunity for the most disadvantaged members of society. If all the Republicans succeed in doing in the civil rights arena is making life fairer for disgruntled white males, they will have lost their last great chance to expand their base to include many of those who benefit little from current civil rights policies purveyed in their name.

"Conservatism comes to power with a stunning lack of moral authority over the issues of poverty and race," declares Shelby Steele. But, he adds, conservatives can win converts among these groups if they compassionately teach the values that the vast majority of Americans endorse: hard work, entrepreneurism, strong education and family stability. Whether there is an effort to teach and bring people along will be the ultimate test whether the [1994] election represented a shift to conservative meanness or a return to Jefferson democracy and the classic liberalism of individual freedom and responsibility. My hope is that today's conservative will turn out to be a classic liberal.[25]

The party of Lincoln has of late lost its moral compass on civil rights. If it rediscovers its direction, the Republican party not only can substantially broaden its base; it can also help America make enormous strides toward fulfilling the promise of opportunity.

# 9. Common Ground

Can our nation once again set itself toward the task of racial harmony? I think the answer is yes—if we rediscover the essential principles and values that lend themselves to that task.

We have made a great deal of progress in breaching the racial divide since 1954. Those who engaged in massive resistance to civil rights were defeated; and more important, their defective ideologies were soundly repudiated. Americans of all colors and races and nationalities were freed from racist dogma to live and work together, to attend the same schools, to marry, to stand on the ground of equality.

And yet in light of all we could have hoped for, we cannot be satisfied. We remain to a frustratingly large extent a racially divided nation, in a betrayal of the melting-pot ideal and the principle of individualism. Much of the blame can be placed on the fact that our government continues to classify us, and to apportion opportunities, on the basis of immutable characteristics. Thirty years after the Civil Rights Act of 1964, our civil rights policies divide Americans along racial grounds, treating people not as individuals but as members of groups, emphasizing entitlements rather than freedom. Those policies exacerbate the tendency to think of ourselves not as individuals, or as Americans, but as members of racial groups.

Perhaps the greatest expression of that tendency came in the October 1995 verdict in the O. J. Simpson murder trial. That the vast number of Americans could sit as jury and assess the same evidence, yet come to different judgments largely along racial lines, underscores that our experiences, and in turn our perceptions, are colored heavily by race-consciousness. It seems obvious we need to create a common American experience, and to stop treating each other as group members rather than as individuals, if ever we are to be a united nation.

Clearly the road we are on is the wrong one. The easy part is recognizing that fact, and I think most Americans do. The harder part is getting back on the right track.

But blocking the road are two interrelated and widely propagated myths that have propped up the failed and divisive civil rights revisionism. To find common ground once again on issues of race and civil rights, we must identify and sweep these myths away.

*Myth No. 1*

Because racism permeates American life, minority individuals will never be able to earn their fair share of the American Dream, and therefore policies that confer benefits and opportunities on the basis of race are essential to minority progress and constitute a litmus test issue for minority Americans.

*Myth No. 2*

Minority Americans hold different beliefs and aspirations than do white Americans, and have cast their lot irrevocably with racially redistributionist policies and with the perpetuation and expansion of the welfare state.

Until recently, neither myth was questioned. The architects of civil rights revisionism often maintain that so much as raising doubt about conventional wisdom is tantamount to fomenting racial division. By this threat they hope to stifle discussion or change. In fact they have the situation backward: it is the policies of color-hyphenation that divide Americans, not the people who advocate the end to such policies.

But can such questions be raised without setting off racial polarization? I think the answer is yes. For thoughtful commentators on both sides of the ideological divide are beginning seriously to question conventional wisdom and to offer tangible alternatives. If the process is allowed to proceed, I am convinced the edifice of race-based policies will collapse under its own weight and we will begin finally to deal constructively with serious social problems that contribute to racial inequality.

The fact is that neither the premises nor the conclusions underlying the twin myths of civil rights revisionism are true. Moreover, though both myths are evoked to justify race-conscious policies, they are logically inconsistent and lead to contradictory results. The first myth (pervasive racism) leads to racial balance policies such as forced busing and employment quotas, while the second (blacks are different) leads to segregative policies such as racially gerrymandered voting districts and separate college dormitories. Those who perpetuate the myths seem to perceive no inconsistency between those disparate goals. Do they want integration or segregation, or sometimes one and then the other? The only options the self-anointed civil rights leadership seems consistently to rule out are racial neutrality and individual choice, precisely the goals of the original civil rights movement.

But the myths have been effective in the political arena. White politicians, whether liberal or conservative, are desperately afraid of being called racists. So typically they accept these myths without question and embrace, in whole or in part, an agenda dictated by those who purport to speak for black America.

But times are changing. A new generation of intellectuals and political leaders is emerging, including whites who are too young to be tarred with the guilt of being on the wrong side of civil rights in the 1960s, and blacks who are calling into question conventional wisdom on issues of race and public policy. Many of the new leaders believe that discrimination is wrong, whether perpetrated against blacks or whites, and that recent civil rights policies have failed to much help the truly disadvantaged.

Those who have the courage to challenge the civil rights status quo will find a strong consensus behind a twofold approach of eliminating race and gender preferences and embracing the common set of values and principles called the American Creed. An examination of the myths of civil rights revisionism leads precisely to that path.

*Myth number one: An incurably racist America.* America is not permeated by racism. By color-consciousness, yes; but that condition—and perhaps racism as well—is exacerbated, not diminished, by policies that divide Americans on the basis of race. Nor, as we have seen, are such race-based policies efficacious in remedying discrimination or its effects.

The crucial first step in restoring a common ground on civil rights is to curb government's power to discriminate. Here a bright-line rule is absolutely essential: as the great civil rights leaders throughout history have recognized, any exception to the principle of color-blindness by government will eventually swallow the rule. For the past 30 years our society has tried to harness government's power to discriminate in a beneficent way, but the experiences recounted in this book demonstrate that the exercise of such inherently arbitrary power is never benign. Moreover, the U.S. Supreme Court repeatedly has narrowed the range of circumstances that justify race-conscious government action, yet preference policies continue to proliferate. Clearly, government's voracious appetite for redistributing power and opportunities cannot be harnessed, and therefore it must be eliminated.

Indeed, this is the lesson as well in other countries that have experimented with racial preferences. Sometimes Americans indulge in parochial assumptions that they are first in everything, good and bad. In fact, racial classifications are an old story, the world over; not just South African-style apartheid, but minority preferences that very much resemble American "affirmative action." And the results are always the same.

Citing economist Thomas Sowell's examination of preference policies around the globe, *The Economist* found four consistently recurrent themes:

> First, colour-conscious policies, like other entitlement programmes, often start out temporary and narrow but wind up permanent and broad.... Second, within favoured colour groups, the benefits of preferments go disproportionately to those at the top, while those at the bottom are frequently left behind.... [T]hird ... is the lack of any clear knowledge about the real-world effects of color-conscious policies.... On a fourth point, the facts are clearer: colour-conscious policies are polarising.[1]

Reviewing the worldwide record, *The Economist* concluded: "To the well-proved principle that separates church from state, another principle should be added. That is the separation of race and state."[2]

For the emerging new generation of civil rights leaders, one credo above all should be sacrosanct: *the principle of nondiscrimination is nonnegotiable.* What this means is enactment of legislation at all levels of government that forbids absolutely the power of government to discriminate on the basis of color, race, or national origin.[3] Such action would require no constitutional amendment or modification of existing civil rights statutes. Indeed, in view of the pervasive race preferences we have today in the guise of civil rights, it may come

as revelation that not a single civil rights law requires racial preferences, and several seem clearly to prohibit them. The new rule of
law would add to these a postscript: *we really mean it.*

This restriction should direct itself toward government, prohibiting it from discriminating and from requiring or encouraging discrimination by private individuals or organizations. The reasons for
aiming the prohibition at government are threefold. First, while the
market is the primary regulator of private transactions, the Constitution and laws are the primary regulator of government. Market
forces that might restrain discrimination in the private sphere are
ineffective in constraining irrational government actions; indeed,
government operates within a political marketplace in which special
interests hold powerful sway. If government is not denied by law
the power to discriminate, political pressures will always induce it
to exercise that power.

Second, and closely related to the first, is that our government is
based on the notion of a social contract designed to ensure the rights
of every person. As the architects of the American civil rights vision
understood, the absolute principle of equality of law is a prerequisite
to securing individual rights. If all our rights are not protected
equally, then none of our rights is really secure.

Finally, government today is a major source of race-consciousness
and discrimination in the private sphere. Before resorting to the
drastic step of further restricting the freedom of association that
should predominate in the private sphere, we should establish a
rule of law in which government is required to act as an impartial
referee, and is no longer allowed to redistribute opportunities on
the basis of race or to coerce others to do the same.

These rules evoke strong popular assent. Opposition to racial
preferences is not fueled, as defenders of the status quo like to
portray it, primarily by angry white males. Indeed, relatively few
people identify themselves as either victims or beneficiaries of racial
preferences. Rather, people (whether white or black) who strongly
oppose racial preferences mainly do so not because they are personally affected, but because preferences so blatantly offend basic American principles of fairness.

White Americans in particular are intensely opposed to racial
preferences, and as Sniderman and Piazza observed in their study
of racial attitudes, the positions on this issue "are markedly firmer,

less malleable than the positions they take on more traditional forms of government assistance for the disadvantaged."[4] As Seymour Martin Lipset explains, "American public opinion is powerfully against discrimination. The general agreement dissolves, however, when compulsory integration and quotas are involved. Many whites deeply resent such efforts, not because they oppose racial equality, but because they feel those measures violate their individual freedom."[5]

Indeed, as Sniderman and Piazza found, race-based affirmative action "produces resentment and disaffection not because it assists blacks—substantial numbers of whites are prepared to support a range of policies to see blacks better off—but because it is judged to be unfair."[6] This obvious departure from basic American principles of fairness explains why there is virtually no gender gap on the issue of racial preferences and why minorities, though descriptively the beneficiaries of such policies, are about evenly divided on the issue. As Sniderman and Piazza found, "Aspects of the new racial agenda are difficult to swallow for many blacks as well as most whites."[7] Moreover, opposition to preferences is especially intense among young people: a recent *USA Weekend* survey of 284,000 teenagers found that nine out of ten are opposed to race-based affirmative action in hiring and college admissions.[8]

For years, polling on these issues has produced consistent results: an overwhelming majority of all Americans (roughly 75 percent) are opposed to racial preferences of any sort, while a slight majority also favors something called "affirmative action."[9] Since affirmative action policies today nearly always involve racial preferences, the reason for this seeming dichotomy is not obvious.[10] I think there are two possible explanations: either respondents think "affirmative action" and the laws requiring nondiscrimination are the same thing (a misperception that civil rights groups eagerly promote); or they support affirmative action (such as affirmative outreach and recruitment) that does not involve the use of race as a factor in making decisions. Either way, a rule of law that forbids racial preferences but allows race-neutral methods to expand the pool of individuals who can compete in the marketplace clearly accords with the popular consensus.

To favor eradication of race-based policies is not to deny the continuing impact of racism. No doubt, racism continues to infect

American society. But the array of civil rights protections seem adequate to the task of identifying and rooting out instances of discrimination, even subtle cases. Preference programs instead supposedly are aimed at "societal discrimination." But as previous chapters have demonstrated, it is increasingly true that racial disparities in areas toward which preferences are targeted—employment, contracts, higher education—are not always a consequence of discrimination. As Sniderman and Piazza argue,

> Bigotry provides a temptingly simple cause for a complex problem; it underlines the moral appeal of working to overcome the legacy of slavery and discrimination by fixing attention on the evil originally responsible for it. . . . There *are* bigots; and although their number is lower now than a generation ago, bigots are in no danger of becoming an extinct species. But to concentrate attention on the deviant and marginal in American life is to miss the larger problem.[11]

After 30 years of second-best efforts to cure the underlying problems, the time seems ripe to try other methods.

Reflexively attributing problems of minorities to racism is costly in other ways as well. Sniderman and Piazza find that the

> charge of covert racism is destructive. Accusations of racism have been leveled so often and so recklessly that the public discussion of the place of race in American life has become politicized and deadlocked. Less obviously, the charge of covert racism has become a handmaiden of a larger argument to call into question the principles of American society. A generation ago, scholars and public commentators saw racism as antithetical to the central values of the American ethos. Now, some researchers see contemporary racism as an expression of these very values. Covert racism is alleged to be commonplace, reinforced by quintessentially American values such as self-reliance, individual initiative, the desire to achieve and to excel—above all, the master idea of individualism.[12]

Civil rights advocates should not be so quick to jettison the movement's traditional adherence to individualism, Sniderman and Piazza urge. For the correlation between racism and people who believe in the tenets of individualism is very low, whereas there is a high correlation between racism and those who are poorly educated or who express authoritarian views toward government.[13] The more educated the respondents in their surveys, Sniderman and Piazza found, the less racist their viewpoints; hence the authors' conclusion, "If one wishes to combat racism, then a lack of education, and the ignorance and simplism it abets, is what one must contend against."[14]

By contrast, it appears certain that race-based policies heighten racial polarization. In their polling, Sniderman and Piazza attempted to determine whether racism fuels opposition to racial preferences, or conversely whether racial preferences fuel racism. They found the latter was true. Opposition to race-based affirmative action has fairly little correlation with negative racial characterizations about blacks[15]; as noted previously, opposition to preferences cuts across racial lines. On the other hand, Sniderman and Piazza found a statistically significant increase in negative white characterizations of blacks after they had been asked about affirmative action as contrasted with situations when the issue had not been raised.[16] The authors conclude that while "affirmative action did not create the problem of prejudice, ... it can aggravate it."[17] The longer such policies perpetuate themselves, the more entrenched the polarization. If we are to move toward racial harmony, we simply must get government out of the business, once and for all, of classifying individuals on the basis of race.

*Myth number two: racial differences.* Even more disturbing is the recurrent notion, purveyed by civil rights theorists, that blacks and whites think differently, that there is a distinctive "black perspective" and even "authentic" blackness. Such notions are antithetical to a society built on individualism, which rejects the proposition that race or skin color determines a person's identity. As Martin Luther King Jr. emphasized, the goal of civil rights is for individuals to be judged not by the color of their skin but the content of their character.

Moreover, most of us, whatever our race, support a transcendent set of values often referred to as the "American Creed." It consists of a belief in individualism, enterprise, equality under law, and basic fairness. It is the glue that holds our society together. Its greatest expression occurs in the Declaration of Independence, and traditionally it has been adhered to by most Americans, whether white or black, immigrant or native-born.

Civil rights revisionism holds that black Americans have abandoned support for the American Creed through dissent from its core tenets of individualism and enterprise in favor of redistribution and entitlements. As Sniderman and Piazza observe, "This reversal of the relation between the American Creed and the new racial agenda is the key to the politics of affirmative action."[18] It would be devastating to our future as a nation if large segments of our society did not believe in the American Creed, and in their ability to earn a share of the American Dream.

Fortunately, this bleak myth is also false. Americans of all colors continue to share basic values and aspirations. It is on this common ground that a forward-looking civil rights agenda can be forged.

Far from holding a monolithic ideology or way of thinking, blacks are fairly evenly distributed along the philosophical spectrum. A 1992 poll by the liberal Joint Center for Political Studies poll found that a slight plurality of blacks—33 percent—consider themselves conservative, while 28 percent are liberal and 31 percent politically moderate. Thirty-eight percent of young blacks (ages 18–34) label themselves conservative.

These conservative leanings manifest themselves in several specific issues, on which common ground exists between whites and blacks. Education is the number one issue for blacks, with 75 percent favoring a "back to basics" approach and 88 percent supporting vouchers to allow parents to choose private schools. With respect to welfare reform, 57 percent of black Americans oppose additional aid for mothers on welfare, and 75 percent believe such welfare caps would deter single women from having more children.[19]

What this means is that civil rights leaders are out of step with many of their supposed constituents on key issues. How little the current civil rights orthodoxy resonates among mainstream blacks was reflected by the lack of response to Jesse Jackson's call for a three-day march to protest the Republican "Contract with America," from House speaker Newt Gingrich's office in Marietta, Georgia, to Martin Luther King Jr.'s grave in Atlanta: only 300 joined on the first day, and by the end the number had dwindled to less than 100, far fewer than Jackson's predictions.[20]

The gulf on important public policy issues between the leaders and the led is reflected in the results of a poll by Linda Lichter, comparing the views of leaders of black organizations with mainstream black Americans. On the question of whether affirmative action or ability should be most important factor in hiring and educational opportunities, 77 percent of the leaders supported affirmative action, while 77 percent of mainstream blacks supported ability over race. Sixty-eight percent of the leaders favored busing for integration, while 53 percent of all blacks opposed it. Two-thirds of black leaders opposed capital punishment, while 55 percent of mainstream blacks favored it.[21]

So, far from throwing off the essential tenets of the American Creed—or the original civil rights vision—most blacks still subscribe to the underlying goals and principles, even if the leadership elite does not. The very tenets underlying the American civil rights vision seem precisely what we need to guide us through the dilemmas we face today—a task to which I devote the next and final chapter.

All this suggests a real opportunity to find common ground on issues of interest to all Americans. No longer should myths guide public policy. Instead we should recognize—and welcome and embrace—these realities:

### Reality No. 1

Racial preferences are divisive and do little to expand opportunities for the truly disadvantaged, and they are a stark departure from basic American principles of fairness and equality under law. A strong popular consensus exists to curb government's power to confer benefits and opportunities on the basis of race or gender.

### Reality No. 2

The American Creed is alive and well, and supported by people of all races. Americans of all races share common aspirations, and it is on the basis of removing barriers that prevent individuals from pursuing their aspirations that future public policy should be directed.

America must quickly acknowledge and act on those realities. The proportion of the minority population—blacks, Hispanics, Asians, and others—has grown from 16.7 percent in 1970 to 24.7 percent in 1990.[22] The percentage of whites is diminishing while others are growing. Blacks no longer constitute a majority of minorities. Interracial marriages blur ethnic lines. All this means an increasingly multiracial society. The course we choose in future civil rights policies will determine whether America in the 21st century is a melting pot or a divided society.

At the same time, serious problems of economic isolation and deprivation persist. While the overwhelming majority of Americans opposes racial preferences, large numbers are convincible—either way—on alternative policies.[23] The danger is that race-based policies will continue to foment racial hostility and diminish enthusiasm for more effective policies.

We cannot afford to let that happen. America needs to make good on its promise of opportunity. We have been diverted from that task for the past 30 years by the siren call of racial redistribution. We can move forward, begin anew the process of racial healing, and eliminate barriers that separate people from essential opportunities—but only if we focus not on what divides us, but on the values and aspirations that unite us as Americans.

# 10. Empowerment

In several of the preceding chapters, I have analyzed the effects of a civil rights agenda grounded in redistribution and racial classifications. It is easy to criticize failed or misguided policies. It is far more difficult to suggest constructive alternatives, but that is the burden properly placed on those who challenge current policies.

It would be otherwise if we were suggesting there was nothing more to accomplish in the realm of civil rights, but in reality much unfinished business remains. Some people contend the civil rights movement is over, that its mission was fully accomplished with the renunciation of the doctrine of separate but equal and the enactment of civil rights laws. They are wrong. So long as arbitrary state-imposed barriers prevent individuals from pursuing happiness, there is more to be done.

In my view, empowerment—the removal of barriers to opportunity that prevent individuals from controlling their destinies—represents the ultimate accomplishment of civil rights. It fulfills the original understanding of civil rights as natural rights held by all in equal measure. Placing it in historical context, empowerment represents the third and final phase of a movement whose first objective was abolishing slavery and whose second was securing equality under law. Empowerment is the necessary culmination of this movement, for even if we succeed in rooting out the vestiges of government's power to discriminate, that will count for little if we are not free.

Imagine for a few moments what our society today might be like if, instead of substituting equality of result for the goal of equal opportunity, as we have for the past 30 years, we had built on the foundation of equal opportunity with an ambitious agenda of individual empowerment. What would have happened, for instance, if instead of imposing forced busing, we had given families victimized by segregation the freedom to choose the best school for their children? Would we have experienced the same intense backlash over forced integration? Would we have had the phenomenon of "white flight" that has decimated inner-city schools and indeed the cities themselves? Would we today have dropout rates among low-income black teenagers in excess of 50 percent and a huge racial gap in SAT scores? What if instead of creating race-specific policies that confer aid on young people who are not disadvantaged, we had given a helping hand to kids who somehow managed to graduate from inner-city high schools in Anacostia or south-central Los Angeles?

What if instead of imposing racial preferences for jobs, we had insisted on adhering to the highest standards of excellence, and had gone about the difficult task of helping people outside the economic mainstream to acquire the tools necessary to compete on an equal basis? What if instead of setting aside contracts for businesses on the basis of race, we had systematically eliminated regulatory barriers to entrepreneurial opportunities that particularly burden start-up companies?

What if instead of arguing that criminal laws discriminate against black criminals, we instead had focused on black victims, and had taken steps to make the streets safe for people and businesses? What if instead of subsidizing out-of-wedlock births and discouraging work, our welfare policies had encouraged work and stable families?

If we had done all these things—if we had stuck with the original civil rights vision and the underlying principles of individualism and equal opportunity—what a different world we might have today. We might have moved toward racial equality without sacrificing racial harmony, toward a society of autonomous individuals judged not on the color of their skin but on the content of their character.

It is not too late.

The task of empowerment requires identifying arbitrary barriers that separate individuals from opportunities, and removing those barriers. As described in the previous chapter, most Americans share basic aspirations: to own a home, live in a safe neighborhood, earn an honest living, and provide good schools for their children—in short, the American Dream.

And yet for millions of Americans, this dream is illusory. Not merely because of poverty: generation upon generation of Americans have overcome economic hardships, and no degree of income redistribution has succeeded in shortcutting the necessary process of education, hard work, and responsibility. But many people, particularly low-income people who live in inner cities, are cut off from basic opportunities. They cannot safely walk the streets of their neighborhoods at night. They are warehoused in drug-infested, run-down public housing units over which they have little control. Prospects for home-ownership are diminished by excessive building codes, zoning restrictions, and other regulatory impositions that add heavily to the cost of housing. Their children are consigned to educational cesspools, operated by self-serving bureaucracies in which barely 50 cents of every tax dollar ever reaches the classroom. Avenues for legitimate entrepreneurship and professional opportunities are foreclosed by arbitrary regulatory restraints. This is not America; it is something akin to Soviet Russia (except the streets were safer there).

The sum effect of these barriers is to make upward mobility nearly impossible for many people outside the economic mainstream. Until we make things right by providing something approaching a level playing field for the most disadvantaged members of society, we will continue to hear pleas for redistribution of wealth and opportunities, based on class or race.

Of all the disabilities suffered by people outside the mainstream, the most personally devastating is crime. Protecting people and property against crime is the first object of government. But for poor people, personal security is a myth.

Civil rights groups tend to focus on alleged racial discrimination in the rates of arrests and harshness of punishments for minorities. Some, including Deval Patrick, have argued that disparate rates of capital punishment for blacks and whites make the death penalty unconstitutional, even though there is no evidence of bias in individual cases.[1] In fact, the concern by civil rights groups for the plight of minority criminals is misplaced. For while blacks are disproportionately represented among those who commit crimes against people and property, they are even more prevalent among the victims of crime. In 1990, 50.8 percent of all murder victims, 30.8 percent of robbery victims, and 33.2 percent of rape victims were black.[2] In the criminal context, the primary civil rights concern should rest not with criminals but with their victims.

Crime in blighted areas has adverse economic effects as well. As Farrell Bloch observes, "employers' reluctance to locate in high-crime areas inhibits the creation of jobs in the inner cities."[3] Moreover, he adds, "many inner-city job seekers live in areas where the drug trade is flourishing and other employment opportunities are diminishing."[4] This means that enterprising inner-city people flock to illicit economic endeavors. "Because the illegal drug trade is highly remunerative, particularly when compared with alternative opportunities for youngsters, it attracts those who would otherwise seek conventional jobs," Bloch explains. "The opportunity cost of selling drugs is the foregone acquisition of skills and experience in legal occupations that could have increased young people's future pay and employment."[5] Moreover, criminal convictions often disqualify young inner-city men from future legitimate endeavors. In large measure a result of drug laws, as many as one-fifth of 16–34 year-old black males and as many as three-fourths of 25–34 year-old male high school dropouts have criminal records.[6]

All this illustrates a skewed environment in which people cannot walk the streets safely at night, and in which many of the most talented entrepreneurs are outlaws. To remedy this perverse state of affairs, government should take several steps. First and foremost, it should rededicate itself to its primary obligation: to protect the security of people and property. The state should ensure the rights of crime victims, including the opportunity to participate in a meaningful way in the criminal justice process and to secure compensation from criminal wrongdoers. It should consider options for community policing, placing the law enforcement apparatus in the hands of people who have a personal stake in the community's security. It should not inhibit the ability of people to defend themselves against criminals, whether by means of private security, handguns, mace, or other methods. And it should repeal victimless crime laws, including most drug laws, that create black market incentives and divert precious law enforcement resources away from crimes against people and property.[7]

Another central facet of empowerment is emancipation from welfare dependency. A system that was intended to serve as a last-resort safety net has become a way of life, draining the spirit from millions of people. The perverse incentive structure—discouragement of work, asset development, and family formation and subsidization of out-of-wedlock births—is catastrophic.[8] One statistic from the first chapter bears repeating here: by the year 2000, fewer than one black child in four will live with two parents.

The welfare system is destroying what slavery and Jim Crow could not: the black family and community structure. (It is steadily eroding white families and communities as well.) We must provide the means of emancipation from the cycle of poverty and dependency. Our public policies must reduce the lure of the welfare state and promote a greater stake in freedom.

A variety of solutions seem to avail. They include caps on Aid to Families with Dependent Children, which reduce the financial incentive to bear children for whom parents cannot provide[9]; "learnfare," championed by Wisconsin Governor Tommy Thompson, which links welfare benefits to school attendance; and devolution of control over welfare benefits to communities and individuals, thereby reducing the voracious and self-serving welfare bureaucracy.

Another escape mechanism is property ownership. Although 64.2 percent of all Americans own homes, only 43 percent of blacks and 40 percent of Hispanics own homes.[10] Repeal of restrictive zoning and planning controls to facilitate construction of low-cost housing, along with tenant management and ownership of public housing, would create opportunities for poor people to gain greater control over their communities and an ownership stake in the American Dream.

Two reforms in particular, which provide a central focus for my colleagues and me at the Institute for Justice, hold special promise: economic liberty and school choice. Both deserve more detailed treatment and provide models for a realistic empowerment agenda.

### Economic Liberty

Like many African immigrants, Girma Molalegne, Rowland Nwankwo, and Ani Ebong came to the United States in search of opportunity. After settling in Denver, they followed the employment path of many other blacks and immigrants, taking jobs as cab drivers.[11]

Before long, the three men discovered a market niche in the poorly served low-income neighborhoods in Denver. Joining with fellow driver Leroy Jones, a transplanted New Yorker, they decided to go into business for themselves as a taxicab co-op called Quick-Pick Cabs. The idea seemed to benefit everyone: improved service for residents of poor neighborhoods, better wages for cab drivers, and opportunities for entry-level entrepreneurs.

But when Jones and his partners filed an application with the Colorado Public Utilities Commission to start their company, they received the same verdict as every other applicant for taxicab permits in Denver had received for the past 50 years: application denied. The result was not attributable to any deficiency of Jones and his partners, but rather the effect of classic protectionist policies, designed not to protect the public but to safeguard politically powerful companies. To start a taxicab business in Denver and in many other cities across the United States, would-be taxicab companies must obtain a certificate of public convenience and necessity—a nearly impossible procedure and one that entrenched interests thwart at every possible turn. Instead of being able to start a low-capital enterprise, thousands of aspiring entrepreneurs are consigned to operate as capitalist outlaws or to work as employees for others.[12] That was precisely the fate that befell Jones and his partners when their application was denied: instead of pursuing their dream of opening their own business, they were relegated to driving cabs for other companies, working in a convenience store, and hawking beer at Mile-High Stadium.

The net effect of entry-level economic regulations is devastating, for entrepreneurship is the most important traditional means for upward mobility in American society. That mechanism is blocked by government-erected business monopolies, occupational licensing laws, and minimum wage and union preference laws (such as the federal Davis-Bacon Act), which are steadily cutting off the bottom rungs of the economic ladder for many minority individuals and low-income people.[13] Rates of self-employment among blacks are less than half the rate for whites.[14] It is little wonder that many young inner-city men succumb to the lucrative drug industry when so many legitimate enterprises are circumscribed.

Leroy Jones and his partners challenged the taxicab monopoly in federal court. They did not seek a handout, or a minority set-aside, or any other sort of special privilege. They sought their civil right to earn an honest living—a right they possess not because they are black but because they are Americans.

But the court turned them away. Of all the rights most Americans think they possess, economic liberty—the right to pursue a business or profession free of excessive or arbitrary government interference—receives the least protection from the courts. No matter how oppressive, economic regulations are routinely upheld by the courts. Thus the anomaly that in a nation doctrinally committed to economic opportunity, today the "right" to a welfare check is much more protected than the right to earn an honest living.

Absent any meaningful legal constraints, regulatory boards at every level of government—often composed of members of the regulated industries—apply the coercive powers of government not to protect public health and safety, but to limit competition from outsiders. As a result, it is essential that in both the legislative and judicial arenas we fight tenaciously to restore economic liberty as a fundamental civil right.[15] We must systematically challenge and eliminate barriers that unnecessarily impede self-sufficiency and economic advancement, and make ours once again truly a society of opportunity. Until we are able to assure that all Americans are free to pursue their dreams—that the rules of the economic game are fair—we cannot with moral assurance resist calls for redistribution and entitlements, racial or otherwise.

The story of Leroy Jones and his partners has a happy ending. Although the entrepreneurs lost the opening round in federal court,[16] their battle was more successful in the court of public opinion. After intense media exposure, the Colorado legislature voted in 1994 to deregulate entry into the taxicab business. Shortly thereafter Jones and his partners filed a new application and secured permits to operate a taxicab business in Denver.

Along the way they changed their company's name—to Freedom Cabs. In defying the odds, Leroy Jones and his partners personified the greatest of American qualities: hard work, determination, enterprise. But the barriers they faced should not be so onerous, imposed on people by their own government. Freedom of enterprise is every American's civil right. And a central task of the next generation in the quest for civil rights is to make good on that precious right.

### School Choice

Of the disabilities inflicted on low-income people, one that it is absolutely essential to change is also the one that it is most within our power to do something about: the public school monopoly. In the realm of schooling, it seems we have tried almost everything: forced busing, massive tax increases, judicial takeovers of school districts, and myriad superficial reforms. The only thing we have not tried is giving parents greater power over their children's education.

June 29, 1995, was an important day for civil rights. Many people remember it as the day the U.S. Supreme Court issued its ruling in *Miller v. Johnson*, striking down a racially gerrymandered congressional district in Georgia (see Chapter 6). But that same day marked another civil rights milestone: two state legislatures, in Wisconsin and Ohio, enacted school choice programs. Although the voting rights decision was trumpeted in newspaper headlines from coast to coast, there was nary a mention in the major media about the school choice developments. Yet 10 years from now, I predict the voting rights decision will largely have faded from memory—we will have dealt with it, and I hope made our nation more racially harmonious for it—but the school choice legislation will be heralded as a turning point in the expansion of educational opportunities for children who desperately need them.

The Wisconsin legislation was actually an expansion of the nation's first school choice program. The Milwaukee Parental Choice Program, enacted in 1990, was the opening salvo in a revolution aimed at effecting a fundamental change in American education and in securing greater opportunities for economically disadvantaged youngsters. Initially, the program allowed up to 1,000 low-income children to leave abysmal public schools and to apply the state portion of their education funds—roughly $2,500 per student—as full payment of tuition in nonsectarian private schools. The program was challenged in court on various state constitutional grounds, and ultimately was upheld by the Wisconsin Supreme Court by a 4–3 vote in 1991.[17]

The choice program brought about systemic change in two essential ways. First, alone among education reforms, the program allowed several hundred children to move immediately from defective schools to good schools. The community private schools participating in the choice program are a far cry from the elite private schools attended by the children of President and Mrs. Clinton and the Rev. Jesse Jackson: they serve primarily low-income, inner-city children, at a fraction of the cost of public schools. The private schools boast graduation rates in excess of 90 percent, compared to 50 percent or less in the public schools.

The reasons the private schools are more effective in serving disadvantaged students are multifaceted, yet simple. Inner-city private schools have little bureaucratic overhead, whereas massive public school bureaucracies absorb about 50 cents of every educational dollar. Although parents have little influence in public schools, they are deeply involved, as a matter of obligation, in private schools. Expectations are high in private schools, and disciplinary rules are clear and consistently enforced.[18]

The second fundamental change results from the fact that school choice transfers *power* over basic educational decisions from bureaucrats to parents, who have the greatest personal stake in the children's future. As a consequence, for the first time, public schools are forced to *compete* for low-income students and the educational dollars allocated for their schooling. Such students routinely are ignored by public school officials because the children have nowhere else to go. But with the spectacle of children walking out the door— and taking their money with them—previously uninterested public school officials must pay attention to the children and address their needs. As a result, school choice can provide a long-overdue catalyst for meaningful public school reform.

The results of the Milwaukee Parental Choice Program are impressive. The children participating in the program are in safe, positive educational environments, in which their parents have significant influence and involvement. The program has drawn not the best or most-motivated students, but rather children who were experiencing either academic or disciplinary problems in the public schools. Ninety-five percent of the participating students are black or Hispanic.[19] Parental satisfaction is high. Children in these schools have excellent prospects for graduation and for college or employment opportunities. Just as important, the program's beneficiaries are leaving the welfare state behind and gaining a stake in freedom.

As a result, the Wisconsin legislature in 1995 expanded the program tenfold and added religious schools to the educational options. The expansion was supported by the Republican governor, Tommy Thompson; the Democratic mayor, John Norquist; nearly all the city's black state legislators; the Metropolitan Milwaukee Association of Commerce; and low-income parents. Similar legislation elsewhere at both the federal and state levels faces more optimistic prospects than ever before.

Still, entrenched opposition is fierce. The teachers' unions, the most powerful special interest lobby in the nation, are militantly opposed to school choice. They have deployed massive resources to fight school choice in every arena: in the legislatures, the courts, and the initiative process. They have challenged the recent school choice enactments in court—with the Institute for Justice engaged in vigorous defense of the parents and children—and the outcome is still to be determined. Every battle over school choice is one between David and Goliath. All of which means that advocates of empowerment must wage the fight for school choice passionately and tenaciously. The stakes are too high for anything less.

Several characteristics are common to all empowerment efforts, whether school choice or economic liberty or any other variety. Empowerment seeks to limit the coercive power of government and to expand individual autonomy. It rests not on notions of paternalism or guilt or victimization or race-consciousness, but on individual liberty, responsibility, and dignity. Empowerment expands opportunities rather than redistributing them, casting civil rights not as a zero-sum game but as an enterprise in which everyone benefits. Most important, empowerment does not divide us but instead draws on the values and principles that unite us as a nation.

Empowerment offers solutions to real problems facing real people—solutions we need desperately to find if our society is to survive and prosper. A nationwide system of school choice would do more to expand educational opportunities for low-income children than any amount of social engineering and public spending. Deregulation of entry into businesses and professions would do more to enhance entry-level economic opportunities than would any number of minority preferences. These are reforms that Americans of all colors and economic conditions can support, if only we have the courage to promote them.

Personally, I would be willing to leave intact the current regime of racial preferences in a straight-up exchange for school choice and economic liberty, for I believe that empowerment of low-income people would render "affirmative action" redundant and obsolete. Unfortunately, no one seriously is offering that choice: the same reactionary forces that support the preference regime usually oppose true empowerment.[20] And in any event, we should not have to be put to that choice. In a free society, the government should not possess power either to discriminate among its citizens, nor to deny them basic liberties. That has always been an essential understanding of the American civil rights movement, and it should continue to guide us into the next century.

The time is ripe for a new direction for civil rights—for well-meaning Americans of different races and colors and ideologies to find common cause to redress the barriers separating individuals from opportunities. To do this requires us to restore and reinvigorate the civil rights vision on which our nation's moral claim is staked. When we do so, I am confident we will discover that what unites us is much greater than what divides us; that we can at last transcend the racial divide; and that we can march forward, together, to fulfill in America's third century the promise of civil rights.

I will conclude my thoughts with an anecdote I have recounted many times in talks and debates around the country. I think it exemplifies what empowerment is all about.

In fall 1991, I argued the first Milwaukee school choice case before the Wisconsin Supreme Court. As we had in the lower courts, we had arranged for a bus to bring low-income children and parents who were involved in the program from Milwaukee to Madison to observe the court arguments. When it was time for the argument to begin, I looked about anxiously: the courtroom was filled to capacity, but the children had not yet arrived. It turned out the bus had broken down and they were late.

When it was my turn to argue, I stood up and glanced at the back of the courtroom. The children had arrived, but there were no seats in the courtroom. So they had to stand outside, their noses pressed to the glass. I thought to myself, what a metaphor: those little children, always on the outside looking in. Yet as a result of the Wisconsin Supreme Court decision upholding school choice,[21] those children are on the inside now.

But that is only the beginning. For with passion, creativity, and an unyielding commitment to principle, a new generation of civil rights activists will see to it that all America's children will live in a land where truly there are liberty and justice for all.

# Notes

## Introduction

1. 438 U.S. 912 (1978).

2. 476 U.S. 267 (1986).

3. John E. Jacob, "Black Leadership in a Reactionary Era," *Urban League Review* 9 (summer 1985): 42–43.

4. Clint Bolick, *Changing Course: Civil Rights at the Crossroads* (New Brunswick, N.J.: Transaction, 1988).

5. Clint Bolick, *Unfinished Business: A Civil Rights Strategy for America's Third Century* (San Francisco: Pacific Research Institute, 1991).

6. Robert Weisbrot, "The Future of Civil Rights in America," *Washington Post* (March 10, 1991).

7. William Julius Wilson, *The Truly Disadvantaged* (Chicago: University of Chicago Press, 1987).

8. Stephen Carter, *Reflections of an Affirmative Action Baby* (New York: Basic Books, 1991).

9. Shelby Steele, *The Content of Our Character: A New Vision of Race in America* (New York: St. Martin's Press, 1990).

10. I urged President Bush to veto the Civil Rights Act of 1991 and instead to champion empowerment policies such as school choice, anti-crime initiatives, and welfare reform. See, for example, Clint Bolick, "Betting on Bush," *National Review* (August 6, 1990): 33–35. See also Chapter 10.

11. Clint Bolick, "Clinton's Quota Queens," *Wall Street Journal* (April 30, 1993); and "The Legal Philosophy That Produced Lani Guinier," *Wall Street Journal* (June 2, 1993).

12. Lani Guinier, *The Tyranny of the Majority* (New York: Free Press, 1994). The book purports to present Guinier's "words in full context and with her own full explanations," *id.*, p. xiii, deleting only "technical footnotes" and "unnecessary passages that are simply redundant" of ideas presented elsewhere. *Id.*, pp. 21–22. In fact, Guinier deleted crucial passages and actually rewrote others from her original law review articles, without acknowledging that she did so. See Clint Bolick, "Lèse Majesté of the Quota Queen," *The Defender* (May 1994); Jeff Jacoby, "Look What's Missing from Lani Guinier's Book," *Boston Globe* (June 2, 1994), p. 17.

13. Despite declaring in response to a question by Institute for Justice communications director John Kramer at a 1994 National Press Club event that she would debate me, Guinier has withdrawn from major media commitments (including CNN's *Crossfire*) after I was scheduled to face her.

14. "Likely Civil Rights Nominee Bashed as 'Stealth Guinier'," *Washington Times* (February 1, 1994).

15. See, for example, Michael Tackett and Mitchell Locin, "Clinton Denounces Critics of Civil Rights Post Nominee," *Chicago Tribune* (February 2, 1994).

16. See, for example, Richard Cohen, "Affirmative Action Under the Gun," *Washington Post* (January 31, 1995), p. A15; Stuart Taylor, "Affirmative Action: Few Honest Advocates," *The American Lawyer* (September 1995): 38.

17. 347 U.S. 483 (1954).

## Chapter 1

1. 347 U.S. 483 (1954).

2. For a discussion of this case, see Bolick, *Unfinished Business*, p. 13.

3. I had the tremendous privilege of defending this program on behalf of participating parents, children, and private schools in *Davis v. Grover*, 480 N.W.2d 460 (Wis. 1992). For an account of the program and the litigation, see Clint Bolick, "The Wisconsin Supreme Court's Decision on Education Choice: A First-of-its-Kind Victory for Children and Families," *The Heritage Lectures* No. 390 (1992). The battle has resumed now that the program has been expanded to include religious schools. The Institute for Justice represents low-income families defending the expanded program in that lawsuit.

4. Quoted in Michael K. Frisby, "Black Family Is Divided on Affirmative Action As Father Backs It, Daughter Seeks Alternatives," *Wall Street Journal* (April 17, 1995), p. A14. For an examination of the human consequences for the victims of race-based affirmative action, see Frederick R. Lynch, *Invisible Victims: White Males and the Crisis of Affirmative Action* (Westport, Conn.: Greenwood Press, 1989), pp. 51–82.

5. Shelby Steele, "Rise of 'The New Segregation'," *USA Today Magazine* (March 1993): 54.

6. Executive Office of the President, Office of Information and Regulatory Affairs, "Standards for the Classification of Federal Data on Race and Ethnicity," 59 *Federal Register* 29831, 29833 (June 9, 1994).

7. Congressional Research Service, "Compilation and Overview of Federal Laws and Regulations Establishing Affirmative Action Goals," *Daily Labor Report* (February 23, 1995), p. E-15.

8. Ellen Goodman, "Black (White, Asian, Indian) Like Me," *Washington Post* (April 15, 1995), p. A15.

9. See Steven A. Holmes, "Bitter Dispute Rages Over Adoption," *New York Times* (April 13, 1995).

10. For an analysis of the discriminatory adoption practices and the applicable constitutional standards, see Elizabeth Bartholet, "Where Do Black Children Belong? The Politics of Race Matching in Adoption," *University of Pennsylvania Law Review* 139 (1991), p. 1163.

11. These decisions culminated in *Adarand Constructors, Inc. v. Pena*, 115 S.Ct. 2097 (1995).

12. Quoted in Albert P. Blaustein and Robert L. Zangrando, eds., *Civil Rights and the American Negro* (New York: Trident Press, 1968), p. 292.

13. See Melanie Kirkpatrick, "Not Black Enough for This Law School," *Wall Street Journal* (January 11, 1995).

14. The division was stark: only 17 percent of blacks would have voted to convict Simpson of murder, while only 18 percent of whites would have voted to acquit. See Joel Achenbach, "The Trial's End, in Stark Black and White," *Washington Post* (September 30, 1995), p. A13.

15. As quoted in James Farmer, "Freedom—When?" in Leon Friedman, ed., *The Civil Rights Reader* (New York: Walker and Company, 1967), p. 129.

16. Quoted in Seymour Martin Lipset, "Two Americas, Two Systems," *The New Democrat* (May/June 1995): 11.

17. *The State of Black America 1994* (Washington: National Urban League, Inc., 1994), p. 20.

18. *The State of Black America 1994*, p. 217.

19. *The State of Black America 1994*, p. 223.

20. Andrew Hacker, *Two Nations: Black and White, Separate, Hostile, Unequal* (New York: Charles Scribners' Sons, 1992), p. 103. In 1964, the black unemployment rate was 9.6 percent and the white unemployment rate was 4.6 percent, for a ratio of 2.09 to 1. In 1990, the respective rates were 11.3 percent and 4.1 percent, a ratio of 2.76 to 1. The gap narrowed slightly during the mid-1970s but has been widening fairly steadily since then.

21. *The State of Black America 1994*, p. 19.

22. *The State of Black America 1994*, p. 232.

23. Hacker, p. 68. Hacker actually places the 1990 figure of black households headed by women at 56.2 percent, compared to 24.4 percent in 1960. The number of white households headed by women also more than doubled during that period, from 7.3 percent in 1960 to 17.3 percent in 1990. Hacker's extensive discussion of related trends makes these statistics even more troubling. *Id.*, pp. 67–92.

24. *The State of Black America 1994*, p. 18.

25. *The State of Black America 1994*, p. 226.

26. Dennis Kelly, "Kids' Scores for Reading 'In Trouble'," *USA Today* (April 28–30, 1995), p. 1A.

27. Shelby Steele, "Rise of 'The New Segregation'," *USA Today Magazine* (March 1993): 55.

28. Farrell Bloch, *Antidiscrimination Law and Minority Employment* (Chicago: University of Chicago Press, 1994), p. 122.

29. Pierre Thomas, "1 in 3 Young Black Men in Justice System," *Washington Post* (October 5, 1995), p. A1.

30. Lipset, p. 12.

## Chapter 2

1. Martin Luther King Jr., "The American Dream," in Washington, ed., p. 208.

2. Robert Pear, "Civil Rights Agency Splits in Debate on Narrowing Definition of Equality," *New York Times* (October 14, 1985), p. A17.

3. Those themes are explored in greater detail in Bolick, *Changing Course*, pp. 5–52.

4. Martin Luther King Jr., *Where Do We Go from Here: Chaos or Community?* (New York: Harper & Row, Publishers, 1967), p. 70.

5. Quoted in F. A. Hayek, *The Constitution of Liberty* (Chicago: University of Chicago Press, 1960), p. 176.

6. John Locke, *Second Treatise on Government* (Indianapolis, Ind.: Hackett Publishing Co., 1980), p. 9.

7. Thomas Paine, *The Rights of Man*, in Harry Hayden Clark, ed., *Thomas Paine* (New York: Hill and Wang, 1961), pp. 88–89.

8. Thomas Paine, "A Serious Address to the People of Pennsylvania," in Robert B. Dishman, ed., *Burke and Paine on Revolution and the Rights of Man* (New York: Charles Scribner's Sons, 1971), p. 198, n. 2 (emphasis in original).

9. Thomas Paine, *Dissertation on the First Principles of Government*, in Dishman, *Burke and Paine*, p. 200.

10. Paine, *Dissertation*, p. 201.

11. Paine, *Dissertation*, p. 197 (emphasis in original).

12. For an examination of the meaning of the Ninth and Tenth Amendments, see Clint Bolick, *Grassroots Tyranny: The Limits of Federalism* (Washington: Cato Institute, 1993).

13. Blaustein and Zangrando, p. 34.

14. Brief for Appellants, *Brown v. Board of Education* (filed November 16, 1953). The brief is one of the most complete accounts of the history of the quest for civil rights in America.

15. Gerald Sorin, *Abolitionism: A New Perspective* (New York: Praeger Publishers, 1972), p. 31.

16. Bolick, *Changing Course*, pp. 14–18.

17. Bolick, *Changing Course*, pp. 18–22.

18. Quoted in Arthur Zilversmit, "The Abolitionists," in James C. Curtis and Lewis L. Gould, eds., *The Black Experience in America* (Austin, Tex.: University of Texas Press, 1970), p. 61.

19. Quoted in "Letters from Santa Fe," vol. III, issue 2 (1994): 4.

20. Blaustein and Zangrando, p. 113.

21. Blaustein and Zangrando, p. 122.

22. Bolick, *Changing Course*, pp. 21–22.

23. *Dred Scott v. Sandford*, 60 U.S. 393, 405 (1857).

24. Quoted in Terry Eastland and William J. Bennett, *Counting by Race* (New York: Basic Books, 1979), pp. 26, 41, 47.

25. *Slaughter-House Cases*, 83 U.S. 36 (1872).

26. For a discussion of the events leading up to the Fourteenth Amendment, the principles embodied in the amendment, and the aftermath, see Bolick, *Changing Course*, pp. 24–32; and more expansively, Bolick, *Unfinished Business*, pp. 54–76. A central mission of the Institute for Justice is to overturn the *Slaughter-House Cases*.

27. See generally Charles A. Lofgren, *The Plessy Case* (New York: Oxford University Press, 1987).

28. *Plessy v. Ferguson*, 163 U.S. 537, 550 (1896). Ironically, that reasonableness standard, which provides deference to legislative bodies to discriminate, is the same standard to which proponents of racial preferences attach themselves.

29. *Plessy*, p. 563 (Harlan, J., dissenting).

30. *Plessy*, p. 559 (Harlan, J., dissenting).

31. Blaustein and Zangrando, p. 316.

32. Bolick, *Changing Course*, pp. 35–36.

33. W. E. B. DuBois, *The Souls of Black Folk* (Millwood, N.Y.: Kraus-Thomson Organization Ltd., 1973), p. 42.

34. James J. McPherson, *The Abolitionist Legacy* (Princeton, N.J.: Princeton University Press, 1975), p. 299.

35. Blaustein and Zangrando, p. 338.

36. For a defense of the role of the judiciary in protecting civil rights, see Bolick, *Changing Course*, pp. 122–41.

37. For an examination of the legal strategies during this period, see Mark V. Tushnet, *Making Civil Rights Law: Thurgood Marshall and the Supreme Court, 1936–1961* (New York: Oxford University Press, 1994).

38. *Korematsu v. United States*, 323 U.S. 214, 246 (1944) (Jackson, J., dissenting).

39. Richard H. King, *Civil Rights and the Idea of Freedom* (New York: Oxford University Press, 1992), p. 13.

40. Gunnar Myrdal, *An American Dilemma* (New York: Harper & Brothers Publishers, 1944), p. 4.

41. Paul M. Sniderman and Thomas Piazza, *The Scar of Race* (Cambridge, Mass.: Belknap Press of Harvard University Press, 1993), p. 129.

42. Eastland and Bennett, p. 108.

43. Eastland and Bennett, p. 109.

44. Leon Friedman, ed., *The Civil Rights Reader* (New York: Walker and Company, 1967), pp. 2–5.

45. 347 U.S. 483 (1954).

46. Brief for Appellants, p. 16.

47. Brief for Appellants, pp. 18, 65.

48. Martin Luther King Jr., *Stride Toward Freedom*, in Friedman, p. 34.

49. For an examination of King's writings, see Clint Bolick, "Everlasting King," *Reason* (July 1991): 54.

50. Martin Luther King Jr., "An Address Before the National Press Club," in Washington, ed., p. 104.

51. Quoted in Richard H. King, p. 101 (emphasis in original).

52. Martin Luther King Jr., "The American Dream," in Washington, ed., p. 208.

53. Martin Luther King Jr., "I Have a Dream," in Washington, ed., p. 217.

54. Martin Luther King Jr., "An Address Before the National Press Club," in Washington, ed., p. 105.

## Chapter 3

1. Quoted in William O. Douglas, *The Court Years, 1939–75: The Autobiography of William O. Douglas* (New York: Random House, 1980), p. 149. The context of the remark was the case of *DeFunis v. Odegaard*, 416 U.S. 312 (1974), the first "reverse discrimination" case to reach the U.S. Supreme Court. The Court dismissed the case on procedural grounds. Justice Douglas, who was adamantly opposed to racial quotas, had looked to Marshall for support, and was gravely disappointed by his colleague's reaction.

2. "Perspectives," *Newsweek* (July 31, 1995): 19.

3. For a meticulous examination of this very question, see Hugh Davis Graham, *The Civil Rights Era: Origins and Development of National Policy* (New York: Oxford University Press, 1990).

4. Martin Luther King Jr., "The Ethical Demands for Integration," in Washington, ed., pp. 123–24.

5. Eastland and Bennett, p. 113.

6. Richard Epstein, *Forbidden Grounds* (Cambridge, Mass.: Harvard University Press, 1992), p. 3.

7. Robert H. Bork, "Civil Rights—A Challenge," *The New Republic* (August 31, 1963): 21–22. Since that time, Bork has turned away from his libertarian beliefs and embraced a philosophy of nearly unfettered majoritarianism. For a critique, see Bolick, *Grassroots Tyranny*, pp. 19–26 and 157–158.

8. Epstein, *Forbidden Grounds*, p. 10.

9. *Legislative History of Titles VII and XI of the Civil Rights Act of 1964* (Washington: U.S. Equal Employment Opportunity Commission, undated), p. 3187 (remarks of Sen. Gordon Allott).

10. Eastland and Bennett, p. 207 (quoting Sen. Thomas Kuchel).

11. Quoted in Morris Abram, "Affirmative Action: Fair Shakers and Social Engineers," *Harvard Law Review* 99 (1986): 1322, citing Hubert Humphrey, *Beyond Civil Rights: A New Day for Equality* (1968), p. 182. Abram is a veteran of the 1960s civil rights movement, and his article offers a powerful moral argument against race-based affirmative action.

12. For a discussion of the evolution away from the principle of nondiscrimination within the civil rights movement during the early 1960s, see Graham, pp. 116–121.

13. Michael Harrington, *The Other America* (Baltimore: Penguin Books, 1963), p. 159. The reader may see parallels to the later book by Charles Murray, *Losing Ground* (New York: Basic Books, 1984), which was derided by the left for its portrayal of an "underclass" that sounds identical to the "other America" described by Harrington. Of course, the prescriptions offered by Harrington and Murray could not be more different.

14. Harrington, p. 162.

15. Harrington, p. 171.

16. Christopher Jencks, *Inequality* (New York: Basic Books, 1972), p. 264.

17. Transcript of "Meet the Press" television news interview, in Washington, ed., p. 381.

18. *The Autobiography of Malcolm X*, excerpted in Friedman, ed., p. 114 (emphasis in original).

19. Stokely Carmichael, "Power and Racism," in Friedman, ed., p. 142.

20. Washington, ed., p. 555.

21. Bayard Rustin, *Down the Line* (Chicago: Quadrangle Books, 1971), p. 115 (emphasis in original).

22. Whitney M. Young Jr., *Beyond Racism* (New York: McGraw-Hill Book Co., 1969), pp. 176, 179, and 183 (emphases in original).

23. Martin Luther King, Jr., *Where Do We Go from Here: Chaos or Community?* in Washington, ed., pp. 615–16.

24. See Graham, pp. 456–457.

25. Rustin, p. 118 (emphasis in original).

26. Abram, p. 1312.

27. 438 U.S. 265, 407 (1978) (Opinion, of Powell, J.).

28. Quoted in Marvin E. Gettleman and David Mermelstein, *The Great Society Reader* (New York: Random House, 1967), p. 264.

29. Quoted in Gettleman and Mermelstein, p. 254.

30. Glenn Loury, "The 'Color-Line' Today," *The Public Interest* (summer 1985), p. 95.

31. Quoted in Eastland and Bennett, p. 7.

32. Nathan Glazer, *Affirmative Discrimination: Ethnic Inequality and Public Policy* (New York: Basic Books, 1975), p. 31.

33. Quoted in Eastland and Bennett, pp. 128–29.

34. Glazer, p. 210.

35. King, *Where Do We Go from Here: Chaos or Community?* in Washington, ed., p. 557.

36. "Where Did the Civil Rights Movement Go Wrong?" *Human Rights* (fall 1988): 22.

37. See Clint Bolick, *In Whose Name? The Civil Rights Establishment Today* (Washington, Capital Research Center, 1988), pp. 21–24 and 54–57. This monograph describes the leading players in the civil rights establishment and their funding sources, which consist heavily of corporate contributors.

38. Bolick, *In Whose Name?*, pp. 22–23.

39. See Bolick, *In Whose Name?*, pp. 28–30.

40. *Statistical Abstract of the United States* (1994), pp. 22–23.

## Chapter 4

1. See Bolick, *Grassroots Tyranny*, pp. 173–74.

2. Quoted in Eastland and Bennett, p. 206.

3. Quoted in Paul Craig Roberts and Lawrence M. Stratton Jr., "Color Code," *National Review* (March 20, 1995): 38.

4. Quoted in David G. Savage, "Battle Against Bias Waged on Shifting Legal Ground," *Los Angeles Times* (February 22, 1995), p. A8.

5. Shelby Steele, "How Liberals Lost Their Virtue Over Race," *Newsweek* (January 9, 1995): 41.

6. Eleanor Holmes Norton, "Equal Employment Law: Crisis in Interpretation— Survival Against the Odds," *Tulane Law Review* 62 (1988): 696.

7. Quoted in Savage, p. A8.

8. Bolick, *Changing Course*, p. 63.

9. Savage, p. A8.

10. See 1995 Congressional Research Service report.

11. 448 U.S. 448 (1980).

12. 497 U.S. 547 (1990).

13. 115 S.Ct. 2097.

14. For a discussion of this strategy, see Roberts and Stratton, pp. 40 and 44–47.

15. 401 U.S. 424 (1971).

16. *Griggs*, p. 426.

17. *Griggs*, p. 430.

18. *Griggs*, p. 432.

19. Section 703(h) of Title VII of the Civil Rights Act of 1964 provides that it shall not "be an unlawful practice for an employer to give and to act upon the results of any professionally developed ability test provided such test . . . is not designed, intended, or used to discriminate."

20. Defenders of adverse impact insist that tests are often inherently biased against minorities. In fact, general intelligence tests, though far from perfect, have a higher correlation with job performance than any other employment selection device. Moreover, such tests tend to overpredict job performance among minorities, meaning that if anything they have a slight bias toward minorities. For a general discussion of this issue, see Clint Bolick, "Legal and Policy Aspects of Testing," *Journal of Vocational Behavior* 33 (1988): 320. See also Lino A. Graglia, "Affirmative Discrimination," *National Review* (July 5, 1993): 28.

21. Lynch, p. 46.

22. *Equal Employment Opportunity Commission v. Sears, Roebuck & Co.*, 628 F. Supp. 1264 (N.D. Ill. 1986), *aff'd*, 839 F.2d 302 (7th Cir. 1988). In a remarkable conflict-of-interest that demonstrates the often symbiotic relationship between civil rights law enforcement agencies and special interest groups, it was revealed that the EEOC

attorney who headed the investigation was a member of the board of directors of the National Organization for Women, which had filed charges against Sears with the EEOC. See *EEOC v. Sears, Roebuck & Co.*, 504 F. Supp. 241 (N.D. Ill. 1980).

These statistical lawsuits, often prosecuted by the EEOC despite the absence of individual victims, remain all too common, and sometimes companies are ruined financially in the process. See, for example, James Bovard, "The Latest EEOC Quota Madness," *Wall Street Journal* (April 27, 1995), p. A14.

23. *Wygant*, 476 U.S. 267, 276 (1986) (plurality).

24. *Wygant*, p. 276 (plurality).

25. *City of Richmond v. J.A. Croson Co.*, 488 U.S. 469 (1989).

26. *Croson*, p. 520 (Scalia, J., concurring in the judgment).

27. *Croson*, p. 520 (Scalia, J., concurring in the judgment).

28. 490 U.S. 642 (1989).

29. *Wards Cove*, p. 657.

30. *Wards Cove*, p. 643.

31. Farrell Bloch, *Antidiscrimination Law and Minority Employment* (Chicago: University of Chicago Press, 1994), p. 50.

32. *United Steelworkers of America v. Weber*, 443 U.S. 193 (1979).

33. *Croson*, p. 519 (Kennedy, J., concurring in part and concurring in the judgment).

34. *Adarand*, p. 2109.

35. *Adarand*, p. 2118 (Scalia, J., concurring in part and concurring in the judgment).

36. John F. Harris and Kevin Merida, "Ruling May Sharpen Debate on Preference Policies," *Washington Post* (June 13, 1995), p. A6.

37. Tony Mauro and Jessica Lee, "Court Blunts Bias Remedies," *USA Today* (June 13, 1995), p. 1A.

38. Bloch, p. 112.

39. Peter Brimelow and Leslie Spencer, "When Quotas Replace Merit," *Forbes* (February 15, 1993): 80.

40. Peter Brown, "Affirmative Action Is Big Business But Nobody Knows How Big," *Scripps Howard News Service* (May 28, 1995).

41. Hacker, p. 103. In 1994, the ratio was about 2.2 unemployed blacks for every unemployed white. Bloch, p. 42.

42. Bloch, pp. 90–91.

43. Bloch, pp. 91 and 94.

44. Epstein, p. 254.

45. Bloch, p. 94. For a further analysis of the economic effects of the Civil Rights Act, see Epstein, pp. 242–266.

46. Alison M. Konrad and Frank Linnehan, "Formalized HRM Structures: Coordinating Equal Employment Opportunity or Concealing Organizational Practices?", *Academy of Management Journal* 38 (1995): 807. See also Jay Matthews, "Reevaluating Affirmative Action," *Washington Post* (July 4, 1995), pp. E1 and E3.

47. Bloch, p. 103.

48. Bloch, pp. 104–105.

49. Sniderman and Piazza, p. 109.

50. Sniderman and Piazza, p. 109.

51. Martin Luther King Jr., "The Rising Tide of Racial Consciousness," in Washington, ed., p. 150.

52. Carol M. Swain, "A Cost Too High to Bear," *The New Democrat* (May/June 1995): 19.

53. Steele, "Rise of 'The New Segregation'," p. 55.

54. For an analysis of those effects in the context of preference programs for women, see Madeline E. Heilman, Caryn J. Block, and Jonathan A. Lucas, "Presumed Incompetent? Stigmatization and Affirmative Action Efforts," *Journal of Applied Psychology* (1992): 536–544.

55. Swain, p. 19.

56. See Complaint in *Jenkins, et al. v. Leininger, et al.* (No. 92 CH 05578, filed Cook County, Ill., Circuit Court, June 10, 1992). The Institute for Justice is prosecuting this lawsuit.

57. Wilson, p. 110.

58. See Steven Yates, *Civil Wrongs: What Went Wrong with Affirmative Action* (San Francisco: ICS Press, 1994), pp. 15–23.

59. Phyllis Berman and Alexandra Alger, "The Set-Aside Charade," *Forbes* (March 13, 1995), p. 78.

60. Helen Dewar, "Senate Rejects Minority Radio, TV Tax Break," *Washington Post* (May 4, 1995), p. A7.

61. "Malicious Murdoch?" *The New Republic* (May 8, 1995): 8–9.

62. Quoted in Steven V. Roberts, "Affirmative Action on the Edge," *U.S. News & World Report* (February 13, 1995): 32.

63. Quoted in Graglia, p. 30.

64. Mickey Kaus, *The End of Equality* (New York: Basic Books, 1992).

## Chapter 5

1. *Hopwood v. State of Texas*, 861 F. Supp. 551, 571 (W.D. Tex. 1994).

2. *Hopwood*, pp. 578–79.

3. *Berea College v. Kentucky*, 211 U.S. 45, 67 (1908)(Harlan, J., dissenting).

4. *Berea College*, p. 69.

5. *McLaurin v. Oklahoma State Regents for Higher Education*, 339 U.S. 637, 641–42 (1950) (emphasis in original).

6. Eleanor Holmes Norton, "Equal Employment Law: Crisis in Interpretation—Survival Against the Odds," *Tulane Law Review* 62 (1988): 696.

7. Quoted in Andrew Kull, *The Color Blind Constitution* (Cambridge, Mass.: Harvard University Press, 1992), p. 173.

8. *Brown*, p. 493.

9. *Brown*, p. 494.

10. See Bolick, *Unfinished Business*, pp. 93–133.

11. Glazer, pp. 109–110.

12. See Lino A. Graglia, *Disaster by Decree: The Supreme Court Decisions on Race and the Schools* (Ithaca, N.Y.: Cornell University Press, 1976); J. Harvie Wilkinson III, *From Brown to Bakke* (New York: Oxford University Press, 1979).

13. *Brown v. Board of Education*, 349 U.S. 294, 301 (1955) (*Brown II*).

14. Graham, p. 372.

15. Michael J. Klarman, "How *Brown* Changed Race Relations: The Backlash Thesis," *Journal of American History* (June 1994): 84. This article provides an insightful recounting of this period.

16. Graham, pp. 370–72.

17. See, for example, *United States v. Jefferson County Board of Education*, 372 F.2d 836 (5th Cir. 1966). For an examination of the metamorphosis from desegregation to racial balance, see Kull, pp. 174–181.

18. Graham, p. 374.

19. *Missouri v. Jenkins*, 115 S.Ct. 2038 (1995).

20. William Raspberry, "The Easy Answer: Busing," *Washington Post* (April 10, 1985), p. A23.

21. *Swann v. Charlotte-Mecklenberg Board of Education*, 402 U.S. 1, 16 (1971).

22. *Keyes v. School District No. 1*, 413 U.S. 189 (1973).

23. *Milliken v. Bradley*, 418 U.S. 717 (1974).

24. *Spangler v. Pasadena City Board of Education*, 427 U.S. 424 (1976).

25. See, for example, *Board of Education of Oklahoma City Public Schools v. Dowell*, 498 U.S. 237 (1991); *Freeman v. Pitts*, 503 U.S. 467 (1992).

26. David J. Armor, *Forced Justice: School Desegregation and the Law* (New York: Oxford University Press, 1995), p. 3.

27. Armor, *Forced Justice*, p. 5.

28. Armor, *Forced Justice*, pp. 174–94.

29. See Bolick, *Changing Course*, p. 62.

30. See David J. Armor, "After Busing: Education and Choice," *The Public Interest* (spring 1989): 24; "Why Is Black Educational Achievement Rising?" *The Public Interest* (summer 1992): 65.

31. For an insightful examination of the failures of the welfare state to create greater equality through income redistribution policies, see Kaus, *The End of Equality*.

32. Blake Hurst, "Runaway Judge," *The American Enterprise* (May/June 1995): 55 (citing a study by University of Rochester professor Eric A. Hanushek).

33. Hurst, pp. 53–56.

34. See *Missouri v. Jenkins*.

35. *Jenkins*, p. 2056 (quoting *Freeman*, p. 489).

36. *Jenkins*, p. 2066 (Thomas, J., concurring).

37. James Brooke, "Court Allows Denver to End 21-Year Busing Experiment and Return to Neighborhood Schools," *New York Times* (September 17, 1995), p. 13. See also Peter Applebome, "A Wave of Suits Seeks a Reversal of School Busing," *New York Times* (September 26, 1995), p. A1.

38. Armor, *Forced Justice*, p. 211.

39. Applebome, p. A21.

40. Dan Beyers, "Diversity's Double Bind," *Washington Post* (August 22, 1995), pp. A1, A8. Since this article was published, the policy was modified but not repealed.

41. Charles Murray, *Losing Ground* (New York: Basic Books, 1984), p. 105.

42. Graglia, "Affirmative Discrimination," p. 28.

43. Hacker, p. 134.

44. See Bolick, *Changing Course*, pp. 66–68. The University of California set aside 16 of 100 medical school seats for members of specified minority groups.

45. See *Podberesky v. Kirwan*, 956 F.2d 52 (4th Cir. 1992).

46. Joseph P. Shapiro, "How Much Is Enough?" *U.S. News & World Report* (February 13, 1995): 38–39.

47. *Podberesky v. Kirwan*, 38 F.3d 147, 152 (4th Cir. 1994) (*Podberesky II*), as amended on denial of rehearings and suggestions for rehearing en banc, 46 F.3d 5 (4th Cir. 1994).

48. Sarah Lubman, "Campuses Mull Admissions Without Affirmative Action," *Wall Street Journal* (May 16, 1995), p. B1.

49. Hacker, p. 140.

50. Steele, "Rise of 'The New Segregation'," p. 55.

51. Hacker, p. 137.

52. More often than I can recount in debates over racial preferences, the presumption is applied that because I am a successful white lawyer, I must hail from a privileged background. In fact, my father had an eighth-grade education. He died when I was 12. I was raised primarily by my mother and worked throughout high school, college, and law school.

53. See Yates, pp. 27–36.

54. The University of Maryland race-based scholarship program was justified in part on the basis of the hostile racial atmosphere at the school and the propensity of students to segregate themselves (see *Podberesky II*, p. 154 and n. 2), which, of course, race-based policies themselves exacerbate.

55. Quoted in Lubman, p. B10.

56. The Milwaukee chapter of the NAACP was lead plaintiff in a legal challenge to the Milwaukee Parental Choice Program, described in Chapter 10. Jesse Jackson opposes school vouchers, though he has sent his own children to elite private schools.

## Chapter 6

1. *Shaw v. Reno*, 113 S.Ct. 2816, 2820 (1993).

2. *Shaw*, pp. 2820–21.

3. *Shaw*, p. 2827.

4. Thomas B. Edsall, "3 Key Justices Question Voter Redistricting Policy," *Washington Post* (April 20, 1995), p. A11.

5. Indeed, the term "gerrymander" is a combination of the surname of Elbridge Gerry, an early governor of Massachusetts, and a salamander, which was the shape of one of the districts that was nefariously created during that time.

6. *Miller v. Johnson*, 115 S. Ct. 2475, 2484 (1995).

7. *Miller*, p. 2494.

8. *Shaw*, pp. 2822–23.

9. Abigail M. Thernstrom, *Whose Votes Count? Affirmative Action and Minority Voting Rights* (Cambridge, Mass.: Harvard University Press, 1987), p. 11.

10. Thernstrom, *Whose Votes Count?*, p. 11.

11. Thernstrom, *Whose Votes Count?*, pp. 18–20.

12. Thernstrom, *Whose Votes Count?*, p. 18.

13. Thernstrom, *Whose Votes Count?*, p. 31.

14. *Allen v. State Board of Elections*, 393 U.S. 544, 569 (1969).

15. *Allen*, p. 586 (Harlan, J., dissenting).

16. Thernstrom, *Whose Votes Count?*, p. 27.

17. See Thernstrom, *Whose Votes Count?*, pp. 38–62; Kull, pp. 216–218; Graham, p. 361.

18. Thernstrom, *Whose Votes Count?*, p. 77.

19. Thernstrom, *Whose Votes Count?*, pp. 137–56.

20. Thernstrom, *Whose Votes Count?*, p. 158.

21. Quoted in Abigail M. Thernstrom, "*Shaw v. Reno*: Notes from a Political Thicket," *Public Interest Law Review* (1994): 39.

22. See, for example, *Miller*, pp. 2483–84. For a general examination of the Justice Department's role, see Thernstrom, *Whose Votes Count?*, pp. 157–91.

23. Kull, p. 210.

24. *Anderson v. Martin*, 206 F. Supp. 700, 705 (D. La. 1962) (Minor, J., dissenting), *rev'd*, 375 U.S. 399 (1964).

25. Proponents of racial gerrymandering argue that the minority districts are not in fact "segregated," because they typically contain large numbers of white voters. Under racial gerrymandering, district lines are drawn to sweep in enclaves of black voters. As the goal is to maximize the number of minority officeholders, racial gerrymandering strives to create majority-minority districts, but not exclusively minority districts, because it will "waste" minority votes to make the districts too heavily minority. By the same token, minority voters will have little impact if they are diffused in heavily majority districts. So while it is technically wrong to call the *districts* segregated, in fact minority *voters* are segregated into majority-minority districts.

26. Clint Bolick, "Blacks and Whites on Common Ground," *Wall Street Journal* (August 5, 1992), p. A14.

27. Lani Guinier, "Keeping the Faith: Black Voters in the Post-Reagan Era," *Harvard Civil Rights—Civil Liberties Law Review* 24 (spring 1989): 431, n. 171. Even though it is essential to fathoming Guinier's philosophy—indeed, it defines her concept of "anti-discrimination"—this passage is deleted from the article as reprinted in Guinier's book.

28. Guinier, *The Tyranny of the Majority*, p. 5.

29. Guinier, *The Tyranny of the Majority*, p. 103.

30. Guinier, *The Tyranny of the Majority*, p. 104.

31. Guinier, *The Tyranny of the Majority*, p. 56.

32. Guinier, *The Tyranny of the Majority*, p. 56.

33. Lani Guinier, "No Two Seats: The Elusive Quest for Political Equality," *Virginia Law Review* 77 (1991): 1514, n. 299. This passage is among those deleted from the article as reprinted in Guinier's book.

34. Guinier, *The Tyranny of the Majority*, chap. 4, 5.

35. Guinier, *The Tyranny of the Majority*, p. 101.

36. Guinier, *The Tyranny of the Majority*, chap. 4.

37. Guinier, "No Two Seats," p. 1484.

38. Lani Guinier, "The Triumph of Tokenism: The Voting Rights Act and the Theory of Black Electoral Success," *Michigan Law Review*, 89 (1991): 1136. This discussion is omitted from the article as reprinted in Guinier's book.

39. Guinier, "The Triumph of Tokenism," p. 1139, n. 298.

40. Guinier and her defenders claim that these theories are merely academic musings, and as she puts it, may not be "realistic, especially within a litigation context." Guinier, "The Triumph of Tokenism," p. 1151. But elsewhere, Guinier is not so hesitant. As Guinier declares in one excerpt deleted from the article as reprinted in the book, "I claim that the interest representation concept is an appropriate remediation principle for sections 2 and 5 of the Voting Rights Act." Guinier, "No Two Seats," p. 1493.

41. *Holder v. Hall*, 114 S.Ct. 2581 (1994).

42. For an analysis of Justice Thomas's opinion in the overall context of Voting Rights Act jurisprudence, see Clint Bolick, "Bad Fences," *National Review* (April 3, 1995).

43. *Holder*, p. 2592 (Thomas, J., concurring in the judgment).

44. *Holder*, p. 2629 (Thomas, J.).

45. *Holder*, p. 2592 (Thomas, J.).

46. *Holder*, p. 2592 (Thomas, J.).

47. *Holder*, pp. 2598 and 2597 (Thomas, J.).

48. *Holder*, pp. 2601 and 2599 (Thomas, J.).

49. *Holder*, p. 2602 (Thomas, J.).

## Chapter 7

1. Much of this chapter has appeared in a previously published article. See Clint Bolick, "Uncommon Ground," *The Defender* (May 1995).

2. National Legal Center for the Public Interest, "Status Quota," *Judicial/Legislative Watch Report* (November 23, 1994).

3. Dorothy Gilliam, "In Black America, What Price for a Clinton Victory?" *Washington Post* (October 31, 1992), p. B1.

4. Thomas Edsall, "The 'Values' Debate: Us vs. Them?" *Washington Post* (July 31, 1992), p. A8.

5. William Raspberry, "Let's Fix It Together," *Washington Post* (November 7, 1992), p. A21.

6. Thomas Edsall, "The Special Interest Gambit: How Clinton Is Changing the Democratic Discourse," *Washington Post* (January 3, 1993), p. C1.

7. Lynne Duke, "White House Tends to Civil Rights Fences," *Washington Post* (June 5, 1993), p. A12.

8. Pear, p. A17.

9. Stephen Labaton, "Affirmative Action Case Embroils Clinton," *New York Times* (April 25, 1995), p. A15.

10. "Appointments Dithering," *Washington Post* (June 14, 1994), p. A20.

11. Ronald Brownstein, "Key Civil Rights Post Left Empty as Search Falters," *Los Angeles Times* (May 22, 1994), p. A1.

12. John McCaslin, "The Lowly Pentagon," *Washington Times* (October 26, 1994), p. A7.

13. Mike Causey, "Defense Adds Hiring Rule," *Washington Post* (September 13, 1994), p. B2.

14. Causey, "Defense Adds Hiring Rule," p. B2.

15. "Memo of the Month," *Washington Monthly* (September 1994): 30.

16. "SEA Says Free Speech is Breached by HUD Cultural Diversity Requirements," *BNA Government Employee Relations Report* 32 (March 21, 1994): 325.

17. Quoted in Clint Bolick, "Coronation of a Quota King at Justice," *Wall Street Journal* (August 31, 1994).

18. *United States v. Board of Education of the Township of Piscataway*, 832 F. Supp. 836 (D.N.J. 1993).

19. See Clint Bolick, "Extortion, Not Enforcement, by the Civil Rights Division," *Wall Street Journal* (April 5, 1995).

20. See Kim I. Eisler, "Say Uncle," *The Washingtonian* (July 1995): 47-53.

21. Jonathan Macey, "Banking by Quota," *Wall Street Journal* (September 7, 1994), p. A14.

22. Jerry Knight, "Lenders Agree to Anti-Bias Pledge," *Washington Post* (September 13, 1994), p. D1.

23. "ABA Conference Takes on Fair Lending," *BNA's Banking Report* 63 (August 22, 1994): 263.

24. Patrick Wehner, "A 'Sea Change' at Justice," *Voting Rights Review* (summer 1994): 3.

25. 59 Federal Register 12606 (March 17, 1994).

26. Edmund Andrews, "FCC Approves Set-Asides for its Wireless Auctions," *New York Times* (June 29, 1994), p. D1.

27. Heather MacDonald, "Free Housing Yes, Free Speech No," *Wall Street Journal* (August 8, 1994), p. A12.

28. Roberta Achtenberg, "Sometimes on a Tightrope at HUD," *Washington Post* (August 22, 1994), p. A17.

29. Carol Innerst, "Education Bills to Get Second Look, Made Local Under GOP-Ruled Congress," *Washington Times* (November 14, 1994), p. A3.

30. "Race-Based Scholarships: Administration Supports U-Md. Program," *Daily Report Card* (October 27, 1993).

31. Roberts, p. 32.

32. Sniderman and Piazza, p. 16.

33. "Firing Based on Race Not Real Affirmative Action," *USA Today* (May 22, 1995), p. 10A.

34. Charles Krauthammer, "Dodging and Weaving on Affirmative Action," *Washington Post* (March 3, 1995), p. A25.

## Chapter 8

1. Bolick, "Betting on Bush," p. 34.

2. Rees, p. 383.

3. For an account of the internal strife over civil rights within the Bush administration, see Charles Kolb, *White House Daze: The Unmaking of Domestic Policy in the Bush Years* (New York: Free Press, 1994), pp. 245–259.

4. See Clint Bolick, "Time for an Omnibus Civil Rights Bill," *Heritage Backgrounder* 827 (April 30, 1991).

5. These arguments were set forth in Bolick, "Betting on Bush."

6. Bolick, "Betting on Bush," p. 33.

7. Quoted in Kolb, p. 250.

8. Rees, p. 391.

9. Clint Bolick, "Blacks and Whites on Common Ground," *Wall Street Journal* (August 5, 1992).

10. Matthew Rees, *From the Deck to the Sea: Blacks and the Republican Party* (Wakefield, N.H.: Longwood Academic, 1991), p. xiii.

11. See Bolick, *Grassroots Tyranny*, pp. 75–76.

12. Rees, p. 277.

13. Graham, p. 475.

14. See Graham, pp. 322–345.

15. Rees, p. 279.

16. Graham, p. 448. For a review of the Nixon civil rights record, see Graham, pp. 301–476.

17. Steele, "How Liberals Lost Their Virtue Over Race," p. 41.

18. Clint Bolick, "The Case for Jack Kemp," *St. Petersburg Times* (March 28, 1993).

19. Bolick, "Blacks and Whites on Common Ground."

20. Source: Hacker, p. 15.

21. Lipset, p. 10.

22. Hart-Teeter, Study #4057 (March 1995).

23. Rees, p. 412.

24. Rees, p. 406.

25. Steele, "How Liberals Lost their Virtue Over Race," p. 42.

## Chapter 9

1. "A Question of Colour," *The Economist* (April 15, 1995): 13. For the insightful study on which the article is based, see Thomas Sowell, *Preferential Policies: An International Perspective* (New York: William Morrow, 1990).

2. "A Question of Colour": 14.

3. I would add gender to this list, but provide narrow exceptions allowing for bona fide gender-based distinctions.

4. Paul M. Sniderman and Thomas Piazza, *The Scar of Race* (Cambridge, Mass.: Belknap Press of Harvard University Press, 1993), p. 145.

5. Lipset, pp. 10–11.

6. Sniderman and Piazza, p. 177.

7. Sniderman and Piazza, p. 130. Specifically, Sniderman and Piazza found about half of all blacks are opposed to forced busing and racial preferences.

8. See William Raspberry, "What Actions are Affirmative?" *Washington Post* (August 21, 1995), p. A21.

9. A CNN/*USA Today* poll in March 1992 asked, "Do you favor or oppose affirmative action programs for minorities and women?" Fifty-five percent (including 53 percent of whites and 72 percent of blacks) were in favor; 34 percent (including 36 percent of whites and 21 percent of blacks) were opposed. An ABC/*Washington Post* poll the same month asked, "Do you think blacks and other minorities should receive preference in hiring, promotions and college admissions to make up for past discrimination?" Twenty-four percent of respondents said yes, 75 percent said no. (By a similar 26/73 percent margin, a majority also opposed preferences for women.) See J. Jennings Moss, "Feelings Mixed on Edge for Minorities," *Washington Times* (March 26, 1995). Within racial groups, the ABC poll found 81 percent of whites and 46 percent of blacks opposed to racial preferences. See Lipset, p. 10.

An NBC/*Wall Street Journal* poll in March 1995 asked respondents about a proposal to end use of affirmative action considerations—such as race or gender—in deciding admissions to state universities, hiring for government jobs, and awarding of government contracts. The poll found 57 percent in favor and 33 percent opposed. With respect to specific preference programs, the poll found only 19 percent in favor of minority-only scholarship programs and 78 percent opposed; 34 percent supported minority contract set-asides, with 59 percent against. Hart-Teeter, Study #4507 (March 26, 1995).

10. As Sniderman and Piazza note, affirmative action is "an empty phrase to many in the public, for whom meaning depends on context." Sniderman and Piazza, p. 130.

11. Sniderman and Piazza, pp. 107–108.

12. Sniderman and Piazza, p. 86.

13. Sniderman and Piazza, pp. 35–87.

14. Sniderman and Piazza, p. 87.

15. Sniderman and Piazza, p. 98.

16. The authors found that 43 percent who had just been asked about affirmative action described blacks as irresponsible, compared with 26 percent for whom the issue had not been raised; similarly, 31 percent for whom affirmative action had been

brought up described blacks as lazy, compared with 20 percent for whom affirmative action had not been mentioned. Sniderman and Piazza, p. 103.

17. Sniderman and Piazza, p. 103.

18. Sniderman and Piazza, p. 130.

19. Clint Bolick, "Blacks and Whites on Common Ground," *Wall Street Journal* (August 5, 1992), p. A14.

20. Thomas B. Edsall, "Disillusioned Rainbow Coalition Mulls Third-Party Bid," *Washington Post* (May 28, 1995), p. A4.

21. Bolick, "Blacks and Whites on Common Ground."

22. Hacker, p. 15.

23. Sniderman and Piazza, p. 178.

## Chapter 10

1. See *McCleskey v. Kemp*, 481 U.S. 279 (1987), in which the Supreme Court by a 5–4 vote rejected this theory.

2. Hacker, p. 183.

3. Bloch, pp. 122–123.

4. Bloch, p. 122.

5. Bloch, p. 123.

6. Bloch, p. 122.

7. See, for example, Bolick, *Changing Course*, pp. 116–18.

8. See, for example, Charles Murray, *Losing Ground* (New York: Basic Books, 1984); Bolick, *Changing Course*, pp. 112–116.

9. A powerful and determined array of special interest groups, led by the Legal Services Corporation, has fought in the courts to create a "right" to welfare and to overturn meaningful welfare reforms. The Institute for Justice is at the forefront of efforts to protect these reforms. See, for example, William Mellor, "Want Welfare Reform? First Fight Legal Services Corporation," *Wall Street Journal* (February 1, 1995).

10. H. Jane Lehman, "Clinton to Seek Higher Level of Homeownership," *Washington Post* (May 27, 1995), p. E1.

11. Indeed, blacks account for 25.5 percent of all taxicab drivers—their second-highest proportion of any occupation (after nursing aides and orderlies). See Hacker, p. 111.

12. See Bolick, *Grassroots Tyranny*, pp. 141–52.

13. See Walter Williams, *The State Against Blacks* (New York: McGraw-Hill, 1982).

14. Hacker, p. 109.

15. A strategy to restore economic liberty as a fundamental civil right is outlined in Bolick, *Unfinished Business*, pp. 47–91. Early successes include *Brown v. Barry*, 710 F. Supp. 352 (D.D.C. 1989), overturning the District of Columbia's Jim Crow-era ban on streetcorner shoeshine stands; and *Santos v. City of Houston*, 852 F. Supp. 601 (S.D. Tex. 1994), striking down Houston's anti-jitney ordinance.

16. The Institute for Justice represented Jones and his partners in the legal challenge to the Denver taxicab monopoly, which was rendered moot when the state repealed the monopoly.

17. *Davis v. Grover* (see Chapter 1).

18. For a pathbreaking and comprehensive examination of the characteristics of effective and ineffective schools, see John E. Chubb and Terry M. Moe, *Politics, Markets & America's Schools* (Washington: The Brookings Institution, 1990).

19. Steven Walters, "Choice Not Siphoning Off MPS' Best Pupils," *Milwaukee Sentinel* (February 8, 1995).

20. Clint Bolick, "The Wisconsin Supreme Court's Decision on Education Choice: A First-of-Its-Kind Victory for Children and Families," *Heritage Lectures* no. 390 (March 25, 1992).

21. *Davis v. Grover.*

# Index

# About the Author

Clint Bolick serves a vice president and director of litigation at the Institute for Justice, which he co-founded in 1991 to engage in constitutional litigation protecting individual liberty and challenging the regulatory welfare state. He served from 1988–91 as director of the Landmark Center for Civil Rights. He previously served at the Department of Justice and at the Equal Employment Opportunity Commission.